George Soros on Globalization

GEORGE SOROS

ON GLOBALIZATION

PublicAffairs Ltd
Oxford

Simultaneously published in the United States by PublicAffairs™,

a member of the Perseus Books Group.

Copyright © 2002 by George Soros.

BOOK DESIGN BY JENNY DOSSIN.

A CIP catalogue record for this book is available from the British Library.

George Soros on Globalization

1–903985–24–2

First Edition

1 3 5 7 9 10 8 6 4 2

Contents

Preface

My goal in writing this book is not only to shed light on how global capitalism works but also to suggest ways in which it could be improved. For this purpose, I have adopted a rather narrow definition of globalization: I equate it with the free movement of capital and the increasing domination of national economies by global financial markets and multinational corporations. This approach has the advantage of narrowing the focus of discussion. I contend that globalization has been lopsided: The development of our international institutions has not kept pace with the development of international financial markets and our political arrangements have lagged behind the globalization of the economy. Based on these premises I have formulated a set of practical proposals that would make global capitalism more stable and equitable.

I was stimulated to embark on this undertaking by what I saw as an unwitting alliance between market fundamentalists on the far Right and antiglobalization activists on the far Left. They make strange bedfellows, but between them they are well on their way to downsizing or destroying the international institutions we currently have. My goal in writing this book was to form a different kind of coalition whose mission would be to reform and strengthen our international institutions and create new ones where necessary to address the social concerns that have fueled the current discontent. Admittedly, our existing international financial and trade institutions (IFTIs)* have some defects; all institutions do. That is a reason to improve them, not to destroy them.

I believe I have some unusual qualifications for this project. I have been a successful practitioner in global financial markets, giving me an insider's view of how they operate. More to the point, I have been actively engaged in trying to make the world a better place. I have set up a network of foundations devoted to the concept of open society. I believe that the global capitalist system in its present form is a distortion of what ought to be a global open society. I am only one of many experts on financial markets, but my active concern with the future of humanity sets me apart from most others. I have spent most of the last five years studying the defects of globalization and have written several books and articles on the subject. My

*I have coined this term to lump the international financial institutions (IFIs) and the World Trade Organization (WTO) together.

last book, *Open Society: Reforming Global Capitalism*,* was rather weak, however, when it came to prescribing solutions. This book is meant, in part, to make up for that deficiency.

I am often told that there is some kind of contradiction between profiting from global financial markets and trying to reform them. I do not see it. I am passionately interested in improving the system that has allowed me to be successful so that it will become more enduring. My interest predates my involvement in the financial markets. Having been born a Jew in Hungary in 1930, I lived through both Nazi and Soviet occupation. I learned at an early age how important it is to your well-being and survival what kind of political regime prevails. As a student at the London School of Economics, I was greatly influenced by the philosophy of Karl Popper, author of *Open Society and Its Enemies*.† As soon as I was successful enough as a hedge fund manager, I set up a foundation, the Open Society Fund (now Open Society Institute), to "open up closed societies, help make open societies more viable and foster a critical mode of thinking." That was in 1979. At first, the foundation focused on opening up closed societies; then, after the collapse of the Soviet empire, on fostering the

---

*George Soros, *Open Society: Reforming Global Capitalism* (New York: PublicAffairs, 2000).
†Published in 1944.

transition from closed to open societies; and more recently on addressing the ills of global capitalism. This book is the natural outgrowth of that engagement.

In trying to build a coalition for reforming and strengthening our IFTIs, I faced a difficulty: It is always easier to mobilize the public *against* something than *for* something. A constructive agenda must be general enough to meet people's aspirations yet specific enough to allow a coalition to coalesce around it. Such an agenda cannot be developed by an individual on his own. Accordingly, I circulated my book in draft form among a broad range of people and asked for their reaction. I received many valuable comments and criticisms, and I incorporated those suggestions that I considered well founded in the finished product. I believe the book in its final version puts forward a constructive agenda that the public could support and the governments of the world implement. The centerpiece of the book is a proposal to use Special Drawing Rights (SDRs) for the provision of public goods on a global scale. The scheme will not cure all the ills of globalization—nothing will—but it should help to make the world a better place.

I was well along in the process of distilling a finished product when the terrorists struck on September 11, 2001. That event created a fundamentally new situation. I felt that the book as it stood then did not go far enough. It was confined to a set of proposals that I considered practical prior to September 11, but it did not spell out the vision of a global open society that has motivated me. The present moment is auspicious for gaining a hearing for that concept. It is not enough to wage war on terrorism; people also need a positive vision of a better world ahead.

September 11 has shocked the people of the United States into realizing that others may regard them very differently from the way they see themselves. They are more ready to reassess the world and the role that the United States plays in it than in normal times. This provides an unusual opportunity to rethink and reshape the world more profoundly than would have been possible prior to September 11.

Accordingly I have decided to add a conclusion to the book outlining my vision of a global open society. It differs in texture from the rest of the book. It is more a polemical tract than a considered report on the deficiencies of global capitalism; more an abstract vision than a set of practical proposals. I intend to elaborate it further in due course. More importantly, the conclusion still needs to go through the critical process to which the rest of the book has already been exposed. Indeed, it needs it more because it discusses subjects about which I know much less than I do about the global financial system.

I was of two minds about including the conclusion

because my goal in writing the book was to build a broad-based consensus, and the conclusion may endanger that objective. The SDR proposal in particular will require the support of the United States to be implemented, yet my conclusion is highly critical of the Bush administration's unilateral, hegemonic approach to international affairs. In the end, I decided to put my trust in the public that I seek to mobilize. People need not agree with all my views in order to support the SDR proposal, and if the public supports it, a democratic government must respect the will of the people even if it dislikes my criticism.

Acknowledgments

This book was written in an interactive manner. I distributed nearly one thousand copies of a "Draft Report on Globalization," discussed its contents at a number of meetings, and received a large number of written comments. Based on this feedback, I revised the text of the report to create this book. I should like to use this occasion to thank everyone who contributed their comments and criticisms, for I found them immensely valuable. Everyone will be able to judge for themselves to what extent I have taken their comments to heart, but for me, the process was both instructive and enjoyable. I take sole responsibility for the final product.

I am particularly grateful to Fred Bergsten of the Institute for International Economics who gathered a highly qualified audience to a luncheon discussion, and to Carl Tham of the Olof Palme International Center in Stockholm, who arranged a panel discussion with Joe Stiglitz, Amartya Sen, Candido Grzybowski, and Susan George on short notice. The Central European University held a three-day seminar on Globalization in Budapest in partnership with the University of Warwick, and I had an opportunity to present my ideas at a luncheon meeting at the Brookings Institution, a meeting of the Group of Thirty, a retreat of the International Monetary Fund Board, a seminar of the London School of Economics, and the initial meeting of the State of the World Forum Commission. The Council on Foreign Relations arranged a small workshop on the Special Drawing Rights (SDR) proposal with the participation of Charles Calomiris, Morton Halperin, Robert Hormats, Roger Kubarych, Geoff Lamb, Karin Lissakers, Allan Meltzer, Edmund Phelps, Benn Steil, Edwin Truman, Paul Volcker, and Michael Weinstein. I also held a number of meetings with government officials, members of Congress and people associated with my foundations.

I have received written or verbal communications from a large number of people, including: Mort Abramowitz, Martti Ahtisaari, Graham Allison, Anders Aslund, Byron Auguste, Terrice Bassler, Michael Ben-Eli, Fred Bergsten, Jagdish Bhagwati, Gavin Bingham, Alan Blinder, Emma Bonino, Jack Boorman, Leon Botstein, Mark Malloch Brown, Michel Camdessus, Thomas Campbell, Geoffrey Canada, William Cline, Robert Conrad, George Cowan, Bob Deacon, Philippe de Schoutheete Tervarent, Joan

Dunlop, Jessica Einhorn, Yehuda Elkana, Gareth Evans, Jonathan Fried, Jim Garrison, William Goetzmann, John Gray, John Grieve Smith, Wilfried Guth, Morton Halperin, Eveline Herfkens, Carla Hills, Robert Hormats, David Howell, Michael Ignatieff, Michael Jendrzejczyk, William Jordan, Miguel Kiguel, Mervyn King, Neil Kinnock, Horst Kohler, Charles Kolb, David Korten, Justin Leites, Jerome Levinson, Anatol Lieven, Mahmoud Mamdani, Paul Martin, Charles Maynes, Federico Mayor, William McDonough, Allan Meltzer, Michael Moore, Bill Moyers, Aryeh Neier, Andre Newburg, Sylvia Ostry, Jim Ottaway, Thomas Palley, Stewart Paperin, Christopher Patten, Maurice Peston, Jacques Polak, Gustav Ranis, Anthony Richter, Dani Rodrik, Alex Rondos, David Rothman, Barney Rubin, Richard Ruffin, Andrew Sacher, Gary Sampson, Robert Scalapino, Tim Scanlon, Pierre Schori, Klaus Schwab, Amartya Sen, Jaime Serra, Clare Short, John Simon, Kiril Sokoloff, Valery Soyfer, Herb Sturz, Daniel Tarschys, James Tobin, Frank Vogl, Lori Wallach, John Williamson, Mabel Wisse Smit, James Wolfensohn, Richard Wyatt, and Violetta Zentai. My apologies to those whom I failed to mention.

Karin Lissakers acted as my advisor and resident expert on SDRs. Yvonne Sheer did much more than type innumerable versions of the text; she coordinated the project and did a lot of fact checking. Peter Osnos of PublicAffairs acted as more than a publisher; he was an integral part of the project. Paul Golob and Robert Kimzey, also of PublicAffairs, managed the publishing part with their usual efficiency. Michael Vachon was in charge of communications. Robert Boorstin provided a critical voice. It was a pleasure to work with them all.

The Deficiencies
of Global Capitalism

Globalization is an overused term that can be given a wide variety of meanings. For the purposes of the present discussion, I shall take it to mean the development of global financial markets, the growth of transnational corporations, and their increasing domination over national economies. I believe that most of the problems that people associate with globalization, including the penetration of market values into areas where they do not traditionally belong, can be attributed to these phenomena. One could also discuss the globalization of information and culture; the spread of television, Internet, and other forms of communication; and the increased mobility and commercialization of ideas, but I am afraid that would take us too far afield. By narrowing the discussion in this way, I hope I can keep it within manageable bounds and produce some practical proposals for institutional improvements.

Globalization as defined here is a relatively recent phenomenon that distinguishes the present day from 50 or even 25 years ago. At the end of World War II most countries strictly controlled international capital transactions. The Bretton Woods institutions, the International Monetary Fund (IMF), and the World Bank were designed to facilitate international trade and investment in an environment of restricted private capital flows.* Controls on capital movements were gradually removed, and offshore financial markets expanded rapidly under the impetus of the oil crisis in 1973. International capital movements accelerated in the early 1980s under Ronald Reagan and Margaret Thatcher, and financial markets became truly global in the early 1990s after the collapse of the Soviet empire.

This is not the first period in which international financial markets have played such a dominant role; similar conditions prevailed prior to World War I. International capital movements were disrupted first by World War I and then by the Great Depression of the 1930s. Clearly, the process is not irreversible.

*The reconstruction of war-torn Europe was an important part of the World Bank's mission. In the end, it was carried out under the Marshall Plan.

The salient feature of globalization is that it allows financial capital to move around freely; by contrast, the movement of people remains heavily regulated. Since capital is an essential ingredient of production, individual countries must compete to attract it; this inhibits their ability to tax and regulate it. Under the influence of globalization, the character of our economic and social arrangements has undergone a radical transformation. The ability of capital to go elsewhere undermines the ability of the state to exercise control over the economy. The globalization of financial markets has rendered the welfare state that came into existence after World War II obsolete because the people who require a social safety net cannot leave the country, but the capital the welfare state used to tax can.*

This outcome is not accidental. It was the objective of the Reagan administration in the United States and the Thatcher government in the United Kingdom to reduce the ability of the state to interfere in the economy, and globalization served their purpose well.

The transformation that has occurred since the 1980s is not well understood. It is not even generally acknowl-

---

*The public sector's share in the Gross Domestic Product (GDP) has not necessarily declined, but the ways in which the funds are raised and spent have significantly changed.

edged.* Capital has always been eager to avoid taxation and regulation, so it is easy to interpret the current tendency to reduce taxation and regulation as merely the manifestation of universally and timelessly valid economic laws. That is, in fact, the dominant view at least in the English-speaking world. I have called it *market fundamentalism*. It holds that the allocation of resources is best left to the market mechanism, and any interference with that mechanism reduces the efficiency of the economy. Judged by the criteria of market fundamentalism, globalization has been a highly successful project.

Friedman, Samuelson, etc

Globalization is indeed a desirable development in many ways. Private enterprise is better at wealth creation than the state. Moreover, states have a tendency to abuse their power; globalization offers a degree of individual freedom that no individual state could ensure. Free competition on a global scale has liberated inventive and entrepreneurial talents and accelerated technological innovations.

But globalization also has a negative side. First, many people, particularly in less-developed countries, have been hurt by globalization without being supported by a social

*For example, *The Economist Survey on Globalization* (September 27, 2001) denies that globalization has reduced the ability of the state to impose taxation and regulation.

safety net; many others have been marginalized by global markets.* Second, globalization has caused a misallocation of resources between private goods and public goods. Markets are good at creating wealth but are not designed to take care of other social needs. The heedless pursuit of profit can hurt the environment and conflict with other social values. Third, global financial markets are crisis prone. People living in the developed countries may not be fully aware of the devastation wrought by financial crises because, for reasons that will be explained later, they tend to hit the developing economies much harder. All three factors combine to create a very uneven playing field.

Market fundamentalists recognize the benefits of global financial markets but ignore their shortcomings. They

*Economic analyses of the impact of globalization yield mixed results. The World Bank's Dollar and Kraay find that developing countries with the biggest increase in trade as a percent of GDP post-1980 have experienced higher and accelerating growth compared to their "pre-globalizing" performance and compared to the performance of "non-globalizing" developing countries. These countries have reduced the income gap with industrial countries. The study found no correlation between changes in trade to GDP and inequality within countries. However, absolute poverty has declined in the "globalizers." On the other side of the debate, Harvard economist Rodrik argues that domestic innovation targeted at domestic investors is a far more important factor in improved economic performance than trade opening. David Dollar and Aart Kraay, "Trade, Growth and Poverty," Development Research Group, The World Bank, June 2001. Dani Rodrik, "The Global Governance of Trade as if Development Really Mattered," submitted to the United Nations Development Program (Harvard University, July 2001).

hold that financial markets tend toward equilibrium and produce the optimum allocation of resources. Even if markets are less than perfect, it is considered better to leave the allocation of resources to the markets rather than to interfere with them through national or international regulation.

It is dangerous, however, to place excessive reliance on the market mechanism. Markets are designed to facilitate the free exchange of goods and services among willing participants, but they are not capable, on their own, of taking care of collective needs such as law and order or the maintenance of the market mechanism itself. Nor are they competent to ensure social justice. These "public goods" can only be provided by a political process.

Political processes generally speaking are less efficient than the market mechanism, but we cannot do without them. Markets are amoral: They allow people to act in accordance with their interests, and they impose some rules on how those interests are expressed, but they pass no moral judgment on the interests themselves. That is one of the reasons why they are so efficient. It is difficult to decide what is right and wrong; by leaving it out of account, markets allow people to pursue their interests without let or hindrance.

Adam Smith said this too

But society cannot function <u>without some distinction between right and wrong</u>. The task of making collective decisions about what is allowed and what is forbidden is left to politics—and politics suffers from the difficulties of reaching collective decisions in a world that lacks a strong moral code. Even the creation and maintenance of markets requires political action. This point is well understood by market fundamentalists. What is less well recognized is that the globalization of markets without a corresponding strengthening of our international political and social arrangements has led to a very <u>lopsided</u> social development.

In spite of its shortcomings, I am an ardent supporter of globalization. I support it not only because of the extra wealth it produces but even more because of the freedom it can offer. What I call a *global open society* could ensure a greater degree of freedom than any individual state. I consider the present arrangements in which capital is free to move around but social concerns receive short shrift as a distorted form of a global open society. The purpose of this book is to identify the distortions and to propose some practical steps toward correcting them.

Institutional reforms are needed in the following areas:

1. To contain the instability of financial markets;

2. To correct the built-in bias in our existing international trade and financial institutions (IFTIs) that favors the developed countries that largely control them;

3. To complement the World Trade Organization (WTO), which facilitates wealth creation, with similarly powerful international institutions devoted to other social goals, such as poverty reduction and the provision of public goods on a global scale; and

4. To improve the quality of public life in countries suffering from corrupt, repressive, or incompetent governments.

The penetration of market values into areas where they do not properly belong also must be addressed. But that cannot be accomplished by institutional reforms alone; it requires a reorientation of our values. For instance, professions such as medicine, law, and journalism have been turned into businesses. I recognize the problem, but in this book I concentrate on institutional reforms.

There is no consensus on the need for institutional reforms. Market fundamentalists are liable to object to the first three points, and antiglobalization activists are strangely blind to the fourth. Bad governments are a major source of poverty and misery in the world today. (Bad location is the other major source, but it is much harder to do anything about that.) Yet antiglobalization activists have failed to give adequate weight in their advocacy to the harm done by bad governments.

Globalization is not a zero sum game. The benefits exceed the costs in the sense that the increased wealth produced by globalization could be used to make up for the inequities and other shortcomings of globalization and there would still be some extra wealth left over. The point is difficult to prove because the costs and benefits cannot be reduced to a common denominator: The GDP is not an appropriate measure of human welfare.* Nevertheless, all the evidence indicates that the winners could compensate the losers and still come out ahead. The trouble is that the winners do not compensate the losers. There is no international equivalent of the political process that occurs within individual states. While markets have become global, politics remain firmly rooted in the sovereignty of the state.

*Amartya Sen, *Development as Freedom* (New York: Alfred A. Knopf, 1999).

[handwritten left margin: EU has made important efforts]

Far too few resources have been devoted to correcting the deficiencies of globalization. As a result, the gap between the rich and the poor continues to grow. The richest 1 percent of the world's population receive as much as the poorest 57 percent. More than a billion people live on less than a dollar a day; nearly a billion lack access to clean water; 826 million suffer from malnutrition;* 10 million die each year for lack of the most basic healthcare.† These conditions were not necessarily caused by globalization, but globalization has done little to redress them.

The inequities of globalization have given rise to widespread resentment and protest. Antiglobalization activists seek to undermine or destroy the international institutions that sustain international trade and global financial markets. Our international institutions are also threatened from the opposite direction. Market fundamentalists are opposed to any kind of interference with the market mechanism; indeed, their hostility to international institutions is even greater than their aversion to government regulation.

[handwritten: Kill the U.N. — misdirect. AID and the World Bank — use corruption to destroy socially responsible governments.]

*Human Development Report 2001 (New York: United Nations Development Programme, 2001).
†Commission on Macroeconomics and Health, *Investing in Health for Economic Development* (Geneva: World Health Organization, December 2001).

The unwitting coalition between the far Left and the far Right has succeeded in weakening the few international institutions we have. The antiglobalization movement has been attacking the IFTIs and particularly the WTO, while the U.S. Congress has been obstructing primarily the United Nations (UN) and only secondarily the IFTIs.

That is a pity. We need stronger international institutions, not weaker ones. We need to form a different coalition whose aim is to reform and strengthen our international arrangements, not to destroy them. The purpose of this book is to propose an agenda around which such a coalition might coalesce.

The institutions that sustain international trade and global financial markets are relatively strong. They do need some reforms because they are being operated for the benefit of the rich countries that are in control, often to the detriment of the poor ones that are at the periphery of the system. But they are more effective and better endowed than the international institutions dedicated to other objectives such as the preservation of peace, social and political development, improvement of health and labor conditions, and human rights.

The UN, which is the most important international institution other than the IFTIs, proclaims its noble intentions but does not possess either the means or the power to translate those intentions into reality. Its noble goals are expressed in the Preamble of the Charter, which is couched in terms of "We the People." But the Charter itself is based on the sovereignty of the member states, and the interests of the sovereign state do not necessarily coincide with the interests of the people who inhabit it. Many states are not democratic, and many inhabitants are not even citizens. As a result, the UN cannot possibly carry out the mission enunciated in the Preamble. It is a useful institution, and it could be made even more useful, but if it is judged by its Preamble it is bound to disappoint. In relying on the UN we must always remember that it is an association of states. As Cardinal Richelieu observed in the seventeenth century and Henry Kissinger has reasserted more recently, states have interests but no principles.* Accordingly, member states tend to put their national interests ahead of the common interest, and that is a serious impediment to the functioning of the UN.

The most powerful element of the UN is the Security Council, because it can override the sovereignty of the member states. Only the five permanent members of the Security Council have veto rights; when they agree, they

*Kissinger quotes Richelieu as having said, "The state has no immortality, its salvation is now or never," which Kissinger takes to mean that states are only

12

Handwritten margin notes: If the states are not the people — what are they? They are the few aggressive individuals who can capture/hold power by force/politics—most can't distinguish between their private arrogant desires and the needs of the people.

Handwritten right margin: not of people

can impose their will on the rest of the world, although this does not happen very often. In effect, the UN combines two institutions within one framework: the Security Council, which takes precedence over the sovereignty of states, and the rest, which is subordinated to it. The need for unanimous consent renders the rest both ineffective and inefficient: The General Assembly is a talking shop, *yes* and the various agencies are hobbled by the need to accommodate the demands of the member states. They also serve as a patronage preserve for superfluous diplomats and out-of-power politicians.*

After the collapse of communism there was a fleeting moment when the Security Council could have functioned the way it was originally meant to, but the Western powers did not rise to the occasion. In the Bosnian crisis they could not agree among themselves, and in the Rwandan crisis they failed to act altogether. In recent years the United States failed to pay its dues and has bypassed or de-emphasized the UN in other ways. Even after September

---

rewarded for might, not for doing right. Henry Kissinger, *Diplomacy* (New York: Simon & Schuster, 1995). In the nineteenth century, Viscount Palmerston said about British foreign policy that, "We have no eternal allies and we have no perpetual enemies. Our interests are eternal and perpetual." Speech in the House of Commons, March 1, 1848. John Bartlett, *Familiar Quotations: A Collection of Passages, Phrases, and Proverbs Traced to Their Sources in Ancient and Modern Literature* (Boston, MA: Little, Brown, 1992), page 397.

*The situation has improved under the leadership of Kofi Annan.

11, the United States has sought to act outside the UN whenever possible. *Because our political leaders think we are gods.*

The disparity between our IFTIs and our international political institutions has rendered the development of our global society extremely lopsided. International trade and global financial markets are very good at generating wealth, but they cannot take care of other social needs, such as the preservation of peace, alleviation of poverty, protection of the environment, labor conditions, or human rights— what are generally called "public goods." Economic development, that is, the production of private goods, has taken precedence over social development, that is, the provision of public goods. This distortion can be corrected only by making better arrangements for the provision of public goods. In this context, it is important to remember that international trade, well-functioning markets, and wealth creation in general are also public goods. Antiglobalization activists are woefully misguided when they try to destroy the IFTIs that ensure these public goods. To "sink or shrink" the WTO would be counterproductive; it would destroy the goose that lays the golden eggs. Instead of agitating *against* the WTO, they ought to be fighting *for* equally effective institutions that would serve the social goals that they seek.

meet to Soros argument

FC

The WTO has decided to engage in a new round of negotiations, to be called the Development Round. This ought to be accompanied by a similar round of negotiations aimed at the provision of other public goods. The needs are well known. The Millennium Summit of the UN, held in September 2000, spelled out ambitious but attainable Millennium Development Goals for poverty reduction, disease control, improved health, and universal primary education by the year 2015. The UN is holding an international conference on Financing for Development in Monterrey, Mexico, in March 2002. That conference ought to focus on the provision of public goods on a global scale. Without it, development is bound to remain lopsided.

The task of the WTO is to facilitate the international exchange of goods and services among willing partners. It has accomplished this task by establishing binding rules and an effective enforcement mechanism. There are two potent reasons why the same approach cannot be used for the provision of other public goods. One is that many countries simply lack the resources to meet international standards and requirements. The other is that it would be difficult to find the kind of enforcement mechanism that works so well in trade, that is, the granting or withdrawing of market access. Instead, there must be some financial incentives to encourage voluntary compliance with inter-

[handwritten margin note: all essential goal, but without population growth reduction, overpopulation will swallow the planet]

[handwritten note at bottom: need a financial incentive]

national rules and best practices. Withholding the incentives can then also serve as a penalty. This could be very helpful in a world where the sovereignty of states stands in the way of imposing rules on individual countries.

It is one of the main propositions of this book that the rules-based system of the WTO for the provision of private goods should be complemented by an incentives-based system for the provision of public goods.

Globalization cannot be held responsible for all our current ills. By far the most important causes of misery and poverty in the world today are armed conflict, oppressive and corrupt regimes, and weak states—and globalization cannot be blamed for bad governments. If anything, globalization has forced individual countries to improve their efficiency or at least to reduce the government's role in the economy. But globalization has made the world more interdependent and increased the damage that internal problems within individual countries can cause. So it is not enough to devise better arrangements for the provision of public goods on a global scale; we must also find some ways to improve political and social conditions within individual countries. That is the second main contention of this report.

Soro's solution

for example! South Africa

The terrorist attacks on September 11 have brought home to us in a tragic fashion how interdependent the world has become and how important it is for our security what internal conditions prevail in other countries. Bin Laden could not have unleashed his attack on the United States without enjoying safe haven in Afghanistan. But the same was true prior to September 11. Ever since the end of the Cold War, most crises that have led to bloodshed were caused by internal conflicts rather than conflicts between states. During the Cold War internal conflicts were exploited but also contained by the two superpowers. After the end of the Cold War the constraints imposed by the superpowers were removed, and the conflicts had to deteriorate into bloodshed before they attracted outside intervention.

This is because outside intervention has been largely confined to punitive actions. Positive inducements have been scarce. After the end of World War II, the United States inaugurated the Marshall Plan, with lasting benefits for Europe. There were no similar initiatives after the collapse of the Soviet empire. Foreign aid amounts to a measly 0.1 percent of the GDP of the United States, compared to almost 3 percent at the start of the Marshall Plan. The progression of foreign aid as a percentage of GDP does not present a pretty picture (see chart 1).

[handwritten margin note, left: Soviet Union was not defeated]

[handwritten margin note, right: Marshall Plan is not a typical situation morally - not a very cogent example]

17

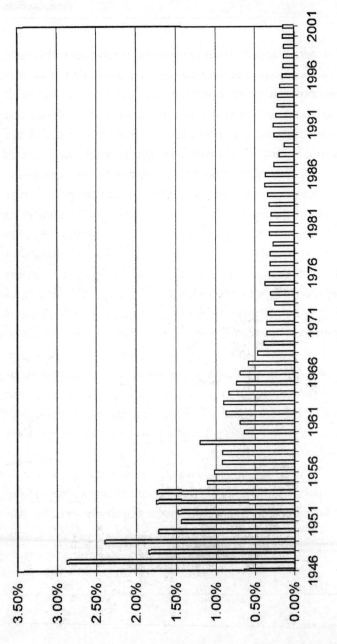

I'd like to see an indication of how much of this "aid" was given to purchase arms from us.

Chart 1: Progression of U.S. Foreign Aid as a Percentage of GDP 1946–2001

Source: The Congressional Budget Office, December 2001.

Preventive action based on positive incentives is much to be preferred to intervention after a crisis has erupted. It is less expensive and causes much less human suffering. Experience shows that crisis prevention cannot start too soon. Early intervention may not grab headlines—it has been said, "a crisis aborted is rarely reported." By the time tensions have led to bloodshed, it becomes increasingly difficult to prevent further bloodshed. Even a country like the United States where the rule of law prevails, is subject to the pressures for vengeance. But in the early stages it is difficult to predict which grievance is going to lead to deadly conflict. This is a powerful argument in favor of fostering what I call *open societies*, where grievances can be aired and institutions exist for addressing them. Conflicts can arise in open societies as well, but they are less likely to deteriorate into bloodshed. It is a vital security interest of the United States and other democracies to improve the quality of governments and foster open societies throughout the world. Fostering open societies cannot take the place of military power, but it can reduce the prospects of having to employ military power.

Democracy and open society cannot be imposed from the outside because the principle of sovereignty stands in the way of outside interference. It can be promoted only by strengthening civil society and offering incentives to governments to move toward economic and political reforms.

see p. 15 →

(1) That poor countries lack resources
(2) a new enforcement mechanism is needed

The two propositions that underpin this book have a common denominator: Both the provision of public goods and the improvement of internal conditions require some resource transfers from the rich countries to the poor. This goes against the grain of market fundamentalism, which claims that markets, left on their own, will ensure the optimum allocation of resources.

ie. rich get richer and poor get poorer.

important to understand these principles.

The resource transfers offered by the existing IFTIs are inadequate. Most of the IMF's money is used to rescue countries after a crisis has erupted. The main business of the World Bank is lending; its grantmaking capacity is largely limited to the profits generated by its lending activity. The WTO is not concerned with resource transfers at all. The IFTIs could play a more constructive role than they do at present—this will be discussed in chapters 1, 3, and 4—but there is a need for a new form of international resource transfer operating along different lines from the existing IFTIs. That is the missing component in the current institutional arrangements. It is the centerpiece of this book, and will be developed further in chapter 2.

It will be very difficult to get the rich countries to engage in resource transfers on an institutional basis. It has been more than 30 years since the Pearson Commission set—and the UN endorsed—the target of 0.7 percent of GDP for official development assistance from donor countries. Only five countries meet or exceed that target;* in 2000, the U.S. contribution was only 0.1 percent, and total official development assistance reached merely 0.24 percent of the GDP of the developed countries. The biggest culprit in the shortfall is the United States.

It is not by accident that international resource transfers are running so far below the 0.7 percent of GDP target or that the United States stands lowest among the developed countries. There is a strongly held belief, particularly in the United States, that foreign aid is ineffective and sometimes even counterproductive. What is worse, this concern is not without foundation.

I feel well qualified to discuss the subject because I have been personally engaged in providing foreign aid on a significant scale—roughly $425 million annually in the last five years—for the promotion of open societies. In that capacity I am intensely aware of the shortcomings of for-

---

*Denmark, Norway, the Netherlands, Sweden, and Luxembourg.

eign aid as it is currently administered. I am convinced, on the basis of my own experience, that its effectiveness and impact could be greatly improved if it were administered differently. Moreover, I am not the only one who is aware of the shortcomings. Serious efforts have been made in recent years by aid institutions, including the World Bank, the Organisation for Economic Cooperation and Development (OECD), bilateral donors, and outside experts, to evaluate and improve effectiveness of the aid, and a new paradigm is gradually emerging.* It is built around giving the recipients a greater sense of ownership and participation in the programs that are supposed to benefit them, as well as reinforcing success.

As I see it, foreign aid as it has been traditionally dispensed suffers from five main defects:

- First, foreign aid serves the interests of the donors, rather than those of the recipients. The provision of aid is often directed by national security interests based on

*The World Bank's *World Development Report 2000/2001*, prepared by a team of development experts led by Ravi Kanbur and Nora Lustig, explores these issues and findings extensively and includes an exhaustive bibliography of the relevant literature. The Bank's Paul Collier and David Dollar have done ground-breaking work and written extensively on these issues. Their key recommendations are summarized in Collier and Dollar, *Can the World Cut Poverty in Half? How Policy Reform and Effective Aid Can Meet the DAC Targets* (Washington, D.C.: World Bank, Development Research Group, 1999).

[handwritten: buy our weapons and attack/resist our enemies]

geopolitical considerations, without regard for the level of poverty or the character of the recipient government. Aid to Africa during the Cold War provides some egregious examples. After the fall of the Berlin Wall, West Germany—eager to secure reunification—gave or lent large amounts of money to the Soviet Union, with little regard for how it was spent. Later, Ukraine became a geopolitical pensioner of the West. Since bad government is the major cause of poverty, it would be far better if donors paid more attention to political conditions inside the countries they support.

- A second, related point is that recipients rarely have ownership of development projects, which are designed and implemented by outsiders. When the experts leave, not much remains. Programs that are imported rather than home grown often do not take root.* Countries like to channel aid through their own nationals—who also act as a constituency supporting foreign aid. Even international institutions prefer to send foreign experts rather than build domestic capacity. The experts are accountable to those who pay them. *[handwritten: yes]*

*Collier and Dollar state bluntly that, "the research evidence is that donors have not had a lot of impact on policy (at least not positive impact)." *Can the World Cut Poverty in Half?*, 21. Many evaluations of multilateral aid and the effectiveness of Fund conditionality consistently conclude that the higher the degree of local "ownership" of reforms, the greater the success. An IMF paper prepared

Nobody, with the exception of my foundations and more recently the United Nations Development Programme (UNDP), is willing to pay for experts who are accountable to the recipients of aid. As a result, recipients often lack the capacity to absorb aid.

- Third, foreign aid is usually intergovernmental. Recipient governments often act as gatekeepers, diverting funds to their own purposes. In some cases, aid becomes the main source of support for otherwise unpopular governments.

- Fourth, donors insist on retaining national control over the aid they provide, resulting in a lack of coordination. When donors compete to deliver aid, it is easier for the recipient government to divert the resources for its own purposes. This was the case in Bosnia, where international aid was largely wasted and served to feed local fiefdoms.

---

for a series of seminars on conditionality concludes, "Policies are not likely to be implemented in a sustainable way unless the authorities accept them as their own and unless the policies command sufficiently broad support within the country." Concerns that "overly pervasive conditionality" is undermining ownership have led the IMF to begin to simplify and reduce conditionality in its programs. See "Conditionality in Fund-Supported Programs—Overview," prepared by the Department of Policy Development and Review, IMF, February 20, 2001, paragraph 14.

Fifth

- Finally, it is not acknowledged that international assistance is a high-risk enterprise. It is much harder to do good than to run an enterprise for profit. That is because there is no single measure of the social benefit, while profits are shown in the bottom line. Yet aid is administered by bureaucrats who have much to lose and little to gain by taking risks. No wonder the results are so lackluster, especially when they are judged by the same standards as other bureaucratic activities and without any allowance for the difficulties involved. It is all the more remarkable that foreign aid has actually produced some positive results in transition countries—for instance in helping central banks, financial markets, or the judiciary to function. This goes to show that in spite of all its shortcomings, foreign aid can be very valuable.

My foundation network works along different lines. Its mission is to foster the development of open societies. Whatever other merits or faults it may have, it is clearly intended to serve the interests of the recipients. To the extent possible, it is managed by nationals of the countries in which it operates. A board composed of nationals decides on the priorities. They work with the government when they can and independently of the government when they cannot; sometimes they are in outright opposition. When foundations can cooperate with the government, they can be more effective; when they cannot, their work is more needed and more appreciated because they offer an alternative source of funding for civil society. As a general rule, the worse the government, the better the foundation because it enjoys the commitment and support of civil society.

confusing – what is the definition of civil society

Open society is often confused with civil society. Civil society is only one of the components of an open society; a democratic government that is responsive to the needs and wishes of the electorate and a private sector that is largely independent of the government are equally important. When a foundation can work with the government, it seeks to improve the government's capacity and make it more responsive to society. Governments that are receptive to that kind of assistance tend to be overrun by donors. But the donors have their own agenda, and the government is capacity-constrained in dealing with them. Some of the most valuable assistance the foundations have given was to increase that capacity by enabling governments to engage experts of their own choosing (and preferably their own nationality).

In addition to national foundations, my foundation network also includes a number of network-wide programs dealing with specific program areas such as education, media, health, information, culture, the justice system, small and medium enterprise development, and so on. These programs operate through the national foundations, but the national foundations can decide whether to participate; if they do, they assume ownership and responsibility for the execution of the programs within their country.* The interaction between national foundations and network programs creates a matrix that combines local needs with professional expertise. The matrix is open ended. National foundations have discretion to operate outside the confines of network programs; they tend to do so in supporting civil society and culture. Network programs may also work with local institutions other than the national foundations; typically they do so in supporting human rights and independent media.

It would be clearly inappropriate to apply the same methods and criteria in a public undertaking as in a private one. Nevertheless the approach of my foundation network could and should be adapted to government-financed international aid. I shall outline how that could be done in

*About 85 percent of my foundation money is spent in the beneficiary countries. By comparison, only 44 percent of the money loaned by International Development Association (IDA) and the World Bank over their existence has been spent in the borrowing countries themselves. *yet these countries still owe 100% of the money. where does the missing 56% go?*

27

chapter 2. My proposal is based on a special issue of SDRs earmarked by the rich countries for international assistance according to certain rules.

SDR = Special Drawing Rights

Governments are unlikely to adopt the SDR proposal on their own; too many bureaucratic and political interests militate against it. But democratic governments are responsive to their electorates. That is why civil society must be mobilized. The time is ripe. The loose coalition of aid activists and church groups known as the Jubilee 2000 movement has fought successfully for debt forgiveness for the heavily indebted poor countries.* The governments of the G7 and the G20 countries are looking for ways to alleviate the problems created by globalization.† The UN's March 2002 International Conference on Financing for Development provides another suitable forum. The terrorist attack on September 11 has made public opinion in the United States more aware of the rest of the world, more receptive to new ideas and more compassionate. If the public demands it, the government can be expected to act.

---

*The movement likened the idea of debt forgiveness to the biblical concept of Jubilee. Pope John Paul II declared 2000 a year of Jubilee.
†The G7 consists of Canada, France, Germany, Italy, Japan, the United Kingdom, and the United States. The G20 includes the major emerging market economies.

Now that is a good use of the Pope's influence

Unfortunately, it is more difficult to mobilize civil society *for* something than *against* something. But the SDR proposal outlined in chapter 2 is concrete enough and reasonable enough to generate broad public support. This cannot be said about the proposals contained in the other chapters concerning the reform of our existing IFTIs. These are more arcane matters that must be dealt with by experts. But public pressure could be effective in calling for the authorities to act.

CHAPTER 1

International Trade:
The World Trade Organization

Economic theory has shown that—other things being equal—international trade benefits all parties. In practice, other things are rarely equal. In particular, the gainers from international trade rarely compensate the losers. Nevertheless, few people would question the benefits of international trade. Individual countries may seek, however, to derive additional benefits by imposing import restrictions or subsidizing exports. The injured parties are likely to retaliate, and if the process goes unchecked, the benefits of free trade are likely to be lost. That is why it is so important to establish general rules by which all parties abide, and that is what the WTO has accomplished. This makes the WTO a very valuable institution. If it didn't exist, it would have to be invented.

The WTO is, in many ways, the most advanced and fully developed of our international institutions. It has been successful not only in creating international law but also in exercising a judiciary function. Moreover, it has found a way to enforce its judgments. The device used by the WTO is to authorize the injured country to retaliate unless it receives compensation or the practice is discontinued. This is a very effective device; in most other areas the sovereignty of states poses insurmountable obstacles to the enforcement of international law.

Because of these features, I have been a great admirer of the WTO—without actually knowing too much about it. In fact, the inner workings of the WTO are so complicated that when it came to discussing the organization, my eyes used to glaze over. But more recently, the WTO has come under concerted attack by a coalition of nongovernmental organizations (NGOs) and labor unions. This has forced me to look at the WTO more closely, and I found that its critics have some valid points.

There is very little wrong with the mechanism itself. The mission of the WTO is the rules-based liberalization of international trade, and it accomplishes that mission brilliantly. Indeed, given the fact that the organization of the WTO required the unanimous consent of the founding members, it must be acknowledged as an outstanding feat of lawyerly ingenuity. Nevertheless, the critics are right in claiming that the WTO is biased in favor of the rich countries and multinational corporations. The bias is due not to the mechanism of the WTO but to the way it has been used, and to the absence of similarly effective structures for the pursuit of other social goals such as the protection of the environment, labor rights, and human rights. I shall consider these two types of deficiencies in turn.

As regards the misuse of the WTO mechanism, two issues stand out. The first, and in terms of the sheer volume of trade most important, is the disparity in the treatment of developed and developing countries' products. The removal of tariff and non-tariff restrictions on agricultural products, textiles, and footware is phased in over a much longer period than on more advanced industrial goods. The advanced industrial countries currently spend some $360 billion a year on subsidizing their agriculture.* By contrast, they spend only $53.7 billion on foreign aid.† The United States also continues to retain the benefits of its antidumping laws, which can be invoked for protection against low-cost imports. These features create a very uneven playing field.**

*Data is for 1999, in *Agricultural Policies in OECD Countries: Monitoring and Evaluation 2001*, Table III.
†Net Official Development Assistance (ODA) by Development Assistance Committee (DAC) members in 2000 was US $53.7 billion; found at www.oecd.org.
**The Bush administration has entered into deals with individual members of

33

The second issue concerns the bias in favor of corporate interests. There are agreements on Trade Related Intellectual Property rights (TRIPs) and Trade Related Investment Measures (TRIMs), but there is no agreement on trade-related labor rights, except prison labor, or trade-related environmental measures. The choice of subjects clearly favors corporate interests. Indeed, it was the attempt to enact a "Multilateral Agreement on Investment" that first galvanized antiglobalization activists into protest and handed them their first victory in stopping it.

There is a WTO rule that prohibits countries from treating physically similar products differently based on how they are made.* This rule is designed to prevent countries from discriminating against foreign suppliers by introducing regulations concerning production methods, but in practice it makes it difficult for individual countries to impose environmental, labor, or human rights standards. Such standards could, of course, be imposed by international treaty, but treaties are difficult to reach and even more difficult to enforce. For instance, the International Labor Organization (ILO) has established an elaborate set

---

Congress to obtain their votes in favor of fast-track negotiating authority. These deals do not augur well for the Development Round. For example, the administration committed itself to withholding some concessions on the importation of textiles promised to African and Caribbean countries.

*Except that products made by prison labor are outlawed.

of conventions, but they are largely ignored. Moreover, if the ILO conventions were observed, they could come into conflict with WTO rules. For example, the ILO has authorized member countries to impose sanctions on Myanmar over forced (as distinct from prison) labor, but ILO members wishing to adopt restrictions on imports of Burmese products in response could be found to be in violation of WTO rules. WTO rules also take precedence over domestic regulations *if* those regulations can be construed to discriminate against the products of other countries.* The lack of international regulations and the obstacles to domestic regulations combine to favor corporate interests.

In the absence of equally binding regulations in other fields such as human rights, labor conditions, health, and environmental protection, the WTO gives international trade supremacy over other social objectives.† In a way, the WTO has been too successful. It is practically the only international institution to which the United States has been willing to subordinate itself. This makes it very pow-

*Countries that have or adopt regulations that are found to clash with WTO rules can be subject to trade sanctions by other members.
†The preamble of the Agreement Establishing the World Trade Organization—like the preamble of the UN Charter—sets out a list of noble goals on which it has so far been unable to deliver. The WTO charter states that trade "should be conducted with a view to" ensuring full employment with rising incomes, while protecting the environment and in accordance with sustainable development.

erful. But free trade and free markets serve only to produce wealth; society also needs some other public goods to survive and prosper. There is an imbalance between private profit and public welfare in the world today, and that is a primary reason why the WTO has come under attack.

The weakness of other institutions cannot be remedied by changing the WTO. The WTO is not qualified to deal with environmental protection, food safety, human rights, and labor rights except insofar as international trade is involved. Although some changes could and should be introduced to make the WTO more cognizant of these issues, the main remedy lies in states, particularly the United States, giving equal support to other international arrangements.

The strength of the WTO is its enforcement mechanism. There are two reasons why enforcement is not suitable for the provision of public goods. One is that the member states will not put up with it. The WTO has found an excellent device that sovereign states are willing to accept because they want the benefits of trade. But that is an exception; states will not accept it in other areas. The rules of the WTO cannot be modified, nor can new rules be introduced, without unanimous consent. China has just joined the WTO: Is it conceivable that it would agree to the inclusion of human rights and labor rights? Would the present U.S. government be any more amenable on the environment?

The other reason is that many countries simply lack the resources to meet international standards. Instead of imposing requirements, it would be much better to provide resources that would enable poor countries to comply with those requirements on a voluntary basis.

Take child labor. Instead of introducing a rule in the WTO prohibiting child labor, we ought to provide the resources for universal primary education. We could then demand that the recipients of support eliminate child labor as a condition of receiving that support. In Brazil a successful pilot scheme called Bolsa-Escola pays subsidies to poor families if all their children regularly attend school. An additional scheme is now proposed that would reward the girls with a savings account if they complete eight grades. This is the kind of scheme that could be implemented on a larger scale with international assistance. This approach would overcome the obstacles posed by the sovereignty of states because the acceptance of support would be voluntary.

Or take the social dislocations caused by the "creative

destruction" of global capitalism.* They create a need for compensation, retraining, and a social safety net. These are domestic tasks outside the scope of the international trading rules established by the WTO. But some countries are too poor to finance the necessary measures; they need international assistance. That is the missing component in our global institutional arrangements. We need to establish a voluntary compliance-based system for the provision of public goods to complement the rules-based system of the WTO for the production of private goods. I shall propose such a system in the next chapter.

In addition to a new framework for aid, there ought to be some changes in the framework for trade. A number of issues stand out: labor rights; environmental protection; intellectual property rights, or TRIPs; Trade Related Investment Measures, or TRIMs; competition, anticorruption, and tax policies; and the organization of the WTO. Some of these issues are included in the Development Round; others must be dealt with in other ways.

Creative destruction is the term used by Joseph Schumpeter to describe economic progress under the capitalist system. *See* Joseph Schumpeter, *Capitalism, Socialism, and Democracy* (New York & London: Harper & Brothers, 1942).

Labor Rights

The disparity in the treatment of labor and capital is an essential feature of the global capitalist system as it is currently organized. Capital moves to countries where it finds cheap labor and other favorable conditions. This helps those countries to develop; a number of them have made remarkable progress. Developed countries lose jobs, but the gains from trade allow new jobs, often with greater value added, to be created. There is also a certain amount of migration, both legal and illegal, to the rich countries to fill jobs that cannot be filled locally. But workers in the countries that offer cheap labor are often deprived of the right to organize and are mistreated in other ways. China is notorious in this respect.

working for walmart or McDonalds

Labor rights were not included in the work program for the Development Round, and now that China has joined the WTO it is unlikely that it will be in future rounds. This suits the corporate interests of multinationals just fine.

Communist workers' state!

There is an international institution devoted to the protection of labor, the ILO. The ILO predates the WTO and in one respect is superior to the WTO: It has a tripartite structure comprising trade unions and employers as well as governments. Its Charter is otherwise almost identical with that of the WTO. It has elaborated all the conventions necessary to protect labor. Like the WTO, the ILO authorizes enforcement measures of an economic character against another member refusing to come into compliance with a report issued by an ILO Commission of Inquiry—very much like a WTO panel. The key difference between the WTO and the ILO is the commitment of the member states. For example, the U.S. government has ratified only 13 of 182 conventions of the ILO, and only 2 of its 8 core labor standards.

argue this issue of P.C.

Critics of the WTO who are agitating for better protection of labor rights are barking up the wrong tree. They ought to be agitating *for* strengthening the ILO rather than *against* the WTO. There ought to be a better balance between the WTO and the ILO. If the member states had the political will, they could ratify and enforce the ILO conventions.

The bureaucracy of the ILO would also need to be energized. It has come to terms with its lack of power and does its best under the circumstances, accumulating information and supporting small-scale demonstration projects out of its tiny budget. Going beyond its accustomed role, it has recently established a Commission of Inquiry on forced labor in Myanmar (Burma), which produced a scathing report, but nothing happened. A recent follow-up reported no improvement.

Because the WTO is so powerful, whereas the ILO has proved so powerless, some critics of globalization would like to give the WTO a greater role in enforcing labor standards. But there are problems with this approach. Many labor violations have nothing to do with international trade and may have no impact on it, for example using child labor to produce domestic crops or prohibiting the unionization of bus drivers. Moreover, the WTO might shy away from sanctions on countries that are not signatories to the ILO conventions. The right approach is to ratify and enforce the ILO conventions. That is where civil society ought to come into play, exerting pressure on governments to do so.

It has been argued that under WTO rules actions authorized by an ILO Commission of Inquiry could be challenged in the WTO. That would be the case if a country imposed trade sanctions against Myanmar (Burma). Unfortunately the argument has not been tested because no country has acted on the findings of the ILO. I believe a WTO arbitration panel would recognize the jurisdiction of the ILO; if not, there would be a legitimate cause for agitating against the WTO.

link the two organizations

The ILO is such a harmless institution that China did not mind signing a protocol of understanding and cooperation with it. This may come in useful sometime in the future, when the ILO will have become more powerful, to put pressure on China to respect the freedom of association. China has an almost inexhaustible source of cheap labor, and its labor is becoming more productive as its economy develops. It will be increasingly difficult for other countries to compete unless labor in China is allowed to reap the benefits of its increased productivity.

Environment, Health, and Safety

Environmental, health, and safety regulations pose some thorny problems. As things stand now, countries are free to introduce whatever regulations they want within their borders, but no country can use trade sanctions to impose its own standards on another country when the imported product is physically the same as the nationally produced one. The only exception to this rule is if there is an international agreement in force to which both WTO member countries have subscribed. This makes it difficult to impose environmental standards on other countries. As the negotiations on global warming demonstrate, international agreements are hard to reach.

In a landmark case, the United States introduced a regulation banning the importation of shrimp caught by a method that did not protect an endangered species, namely turtles. The regulation was challenged in the WTO, and after protracted litigation an arbitration panel ruled in June 2001 in favor of the U.S. shrimp import ban, noting in part U.S. good faith efforts to negotiate a turtle protection treaty. This is an important victory for environmentalists and removes a major source of complaint against the WTO; it constitutes a precedent that can be used in other environmental cases.

Many questions remain. Clearly, when a country is affected by production methods in other countries, as in the case of global warming, it should be able to protect itself by imposing trade sanctions. But what if a country is not affected, for example, if leather tanning poisons the air in India or copper refining poisons the soil in Chile? If the United States imposed a ban on Arctic exploration in the United States, could it also ban the importation of Arctic oil from Russia?

Admittedly, the WTO is ill suited to deal with environmental, health, and food issues. The WTO has neither credibility nor expertise in these areas. The issues are complex and highly charged. The WTO has become involved only to prevent them from being used for protectionist purposes. It would be much better to deal with these issues outside the confines of the WTO.

Environmental activists in the developed world are clamoring for universal environmental standards, but poor countries cannot afford to meet those standards. Imposing standards by using an enforcement mechanism would clearly discriminate against the less-developed world. This is a case in which financial incentives should be used to secure voluntary compliance. Protecting the environment is a noble goal; those who believe in it must be prepared to pay for it. There are already many private initiatives for the preservation of flora and fauna; where global concerns are involved, such as the rain forests or endangered species, some public financing may be justified. *It seems clear that Soros does not comprehend the threat.*

There is no general agreement on environmental issues. It has been suggested that something like a World Environmental Organization is needed, but there is such an aversion to international institutions that the call is likely to go unanswered. Indeed, it would be inappropriate to set up a full-fledged bureaucracy, especially if it is not given any

better to ruin nature? yes

authority, but it is not too much to ask for a virtual institution that relies on panels of experts rather than bureaucrats appointed by patronage. Such an institution could gain authority through its expertise and influence global environmental policy. *What about global warming treaty.*

It would be much easier to introduce labor, environmental, and human rights considerations into the hemispheric free trade area proposed by the Bush administration than to retrofit the WTO. The recent change in North Atlantic Free Trade Agreement (NAFTA) rules to make it easier to maintain national environmental standards indicates that popular sentiment is beginning to have an impact on official attitudes about trade policy.* Organized labor remains very suspicious, however, and with good reason: In the case of NAFTA there is no legal bridge between the labor side agreement and the main body of NAFTA; hence a violation of the side agreement has no effect on NAFTA. By contrast, Chapter 11 of NAFTA, the Investment Chapter, has effective provisions for the protection of corporate property rights.

*See "Nafta Deal Changed to Curb Companies," *Financial Times* (U.S. ed.), August 3, 2001, page 3.

INTELLECTUAL PROPERTY RIGHTS

Intellectual property rights raise both conceptual and practical issues. The very expression "intellectual property" is misleading because it rests on a false analogy with tangible property.* An essential feature of tangible property is that its value derives from the use that the owner makes of it, but intellectual property derives its value from the use that others make of it: Authors want their works read, inventors want their inventions used. Patents and copyrights serve to ensure that the creators are rewarded, but money is not necessarily the only kind of reward they seek. For instance, pure science has traditionally belonged to the public domain, and scientists have sought intellectual recognition rather than financial rewards. The establishment of patents and intellectual property rights has helped to turn intellectual activity into business activity, and business is of course motivated by profit. It can be argued that the process has gone too far. Patent protection is of course necessary to encourage investment in research, but something is lost when science, culture, and art become dominated by the profit motive.

To understand what is happening, we have to go back to

*John Kay, "Intellectual Rights and Wrongs," *Financial Times* (U.S. ed.), March 21, 2001, page 17.

the enclosure movement in agriculture. At the dawn of capitalism in England, communally owned pasture was converted into private property to increase its productivity. It is an unfortunate fact that individuals do not derive sufficient benefit from the improvement of public property to justify their making an investment in improving it. This is known as "the tragedy of the commons." Science and culture, which have historically belonged largely to the public domain, now face a similar enclosure movement. The privatization of the public domain poses a potent threat to cultural diversity, indeed to culture itself. It is difficult to imagine how culture could propagate itself without allowing freeriders access to intellectual property. This problem goes far beyond the capacity of the WTO to resolve. To create a better balance between the private and public sphere would require a change of heart and far-reaching institutional changes.

The problems connected with intellectual property rights came to the fore in connection with drugs needed for the treatment of infectious diseases, particularly HIV/AIDS in Africa. Under tremendous pressure from public opinion, the drug companies have begun to yield, and the United States, in a major concession, allowed the issue to be included in the Development Round. So far so good. But the next likely step is that drug companies will redirect

[handwritten marginalia: underemployment.]

[handwritten marginalia: I hate to be cruel + blunt, but the worst disease in the poor countries is overpopulation and]

their resources to less sensitive and therefore more profitable areas. Already far more money is spent on developing cosmetics than on curing tropical diseases.* New incentives will have to be established to foster research and production of drugs for less-developed countries. The Gates Foundation is on the right track when it offers financial rewards for vaccines and other cures for infectious diseases.

The WTO opened up a Pandora's box when it became involved in intellectual property rights. If intellectual property rights are a fit subject for the WTO, why not labor rights, or human rights? There is a need for patent and copyright protection, but such protection does constitute a restraint of trade. How much restraint is justified? The calculus is quite different for technologically advanced countries that profit from innovations and less-developed countries that have to pay for them. Intellectual property rights were high on the U.S. agenda, and less-developed countries have reason to be resentful about the shape that TRIPs took. The subject requires a more thorough reconsideration than is envisioned for the Development Round.

*According to Médecins Sans Frontières, of 1,223 new medicines brought to market between 1975 and 1997, only 13 were for the treatment of the tropical diseases that least-developed countries most commonly face.

INVESTMENT PROTECTION
AND ANTICORRUPTION MEASURES

Another major area of contention is the agreement on Trade Related Investment Measures (TRIMs). TRIMs are designed to provide a level playing field between foreign and domestic enterprises. On the face of it, this is a worthy objective. But the fact is that in a world in which capital is free to move about, the playing field is heavily tilted in favor of international investors and multinational corporations. TRIMs institutionalize and reinforce the bias.

Countries often offer tax incentives and other subsidies to transnational corporations because they have to compete with one another to attract foreign investment. When it comes to the exploitation of natural resources, the concessions are often bought by bribery. Mining and oil companies are eager to fight corruption once they have obtained a concession, but in fighting for concessions no holds are barred.* The WTO has made no attempt to address these issues. TRIMs are designed to prevent trade-related discrimination against transnational corporations. The rules that emerged from the Uruguay Round target domestic-content requirements and export performance require-

*Based on a discussion with high-powered mining company executives.

ments used by many developing countries.* On the other hand, escalating use by developed countries of high domestic content rules-of-origin in regional trade arrangements such as NAFTA and the European Union (EU), locational incentives, and discriminatory antidumping regulations go unchecked by TRIMs' rules. This imbalance must be corrected in the next trade round. There are also no WTO rules against the activities of transnationals that are harmful to the countries in which they operate.

It is difficult to see how the structure of the WTO could be amended to address the issue of bribery. This does not make the issue less pressing. The remedies lie elsewhere, but they need to be pursued with vigor. Some progress has already been made. The United States criminalized the bribery of foreign governments by U.S. companies 25 years ago, and more recently the OECD agreed on an anticorruption code. Additional measures are needed. For instance, the Securities and Exchange Commission (SEC) could impose a requirement on oil and natural resource companies that they disclose the payments made to individual countries, whether inside or outside, if they want their shares traded in the United States. It would then be possible to add up all the payments and hold the recipient

*The Uruguay Round of negotiations under the General Agreement on Tariffs and Trade (GATT) led to the establishment of the WTO.

governments accountable. An NGO called Global Witness has begun to agitate for such a measure, and it deserves support.

There is a case to be made for encouraging home-grown small and medium enterprises (SMEs). That case is not recognized by TRIMs as it currently stands. The trade rules should give room for such support. Again, the incentives would be best provided outside the confines of the WTO in the form of microcredit and better financing for SMEs. This will form part of the missing component discussed in the next chapter.

COMPETITION AND TAX POLICY

The conclusion that trade benefits all parties is based on equilibrium theory. But equilibrium is a static concept, whereas economic development is dynamic. Free markets tend toward equilibrium only when the law of diminishing returns is in operation, but there are situations involving technological innovations and market dominance where additional investment may produce increasing returns. In these cases it pays to push investments beyond the theoretical equilibrium. In addition, countries have to compete to attract capital. These considerations show a need for setting rules against anticompetitive practices at the global level.

Competition policy and some tax issues have in fact been included in later stages of the Development Round. This can be justified on the grounds that if you throw everything into a pot it may be possible to cook up something. It is difficult to see, however, what will come out of the negotiations, given the very different perspectives held by the main trading partners. Taxing capital and curbing the monopolistic aspirations of multinational companies are undoubtedly two of the most challenging tasks of our age.

The advisory panel of finance experts commissioned by the UN Secretary General to help prepare the UN's March 2002 summit on Financing for Development in Mexico, chaired by former Mexican President Zedillo, included in its recommendations the setting up of an international tax organization. This may be too ambitious; there is a strong prevailing sentiment against setting up new organizations. The OECD has been active in the field of taxation and came up with some modest proposals for cooperation. The Bush administration at first resisted them, but changed its attitude after September 11. Progress on controlling tax havens may be one of the beneficial side effects of the war on terrorism.

ORGANIZATIONAL ISSUES

Although I have found very little wrong with the structure of the WTO, there are grounds for criticizing the way the structure has been used. The WTO has been accused of operating behind closed doors, favoring the interests of transnational corporations and disregarding those of the less-developed countries. To a large extent, these faults can be attributed to the way the WTO operates. The WTO has a small staff and a minuscule budget.* This stands in stark contrast to the earlier generations of international institutions and reflects the anti-institutional bias of our age. Although in some ways attractive, the arrangement has some serious drawbacks.

The WTO simply does not have the staff or the budget to maintain adequate communications or to protect the interests of all its members. In the other IFTIs, the staff

*After Seattle, WTO head Mike Moore pointed out that the annual budget of the World Wildlife Foundation ($350 million in 2000) is three times larger than that of the WTO.

elaborates the issues and the negotiating options, and in addition the delegations of developed countries take less-developed countries under their wings; in the WTO, all negotiations are carried on between countries, and the less-developed countries often do not have the capacity to protect their interests. They did not have much say in designing the provisions of the Uruguay Round, yet they had to buy into them wholesale because under WTO rules a country must be a party to all the negotiated agreements as a single package. This may have been necessary to get the Uruguay Round accomplished, but it has given rise to the complaint that many countries did not know what they were signing. Some are having difficulties fulfilling their obligations.

What can be done to correct the situation? Clearly, the capacity of developing countries to participate more effectively in WTO negotiations and decisions must be strengthened. Since I am not sufficiently well versed in the intricacies of the WTO, I shall refer to the British White Paper on International Development* and the Zedillo Report, commissioned by the Secretary General of the

*"Eliminating World Poverty: Making Globalisation Work for the Poor." White Paper on International Development (Presented to the British Parliament by the Secretary of State for International Development by Command of Her Majesty, December 2000); www.globalisation.gov.uk.

UN. These recommend legal aid to help developing countries navigate existing trade rules, technical assistance to build up trade negotiating capacity of the poorer WTO members, flexibility on WTO deadlines, more refined special and differential treatment for countries at different stages of development, and possible reform of the negotiating process. It is encouraging that the Doha ministerial declaration inaugurating the Development Round in November 2001 promises a significant effort to implement these proposals. The British government has also been providing financial assistance to developing countries for this purpose.

In conclusion, the Development Round could be helpful in curing the ills of globalization provided it is complemented by a set of financial incentives for voluntary compliance with international rules and standards. The next chapter proposes a way to provide the missing component.

CHAPTER 2

International Aid:
The Missing Component

The missing component in the international financial architecture is an effective method of providing aid that will enable, encourage, and reinforce voluntary compliance with international standards and requirements. The arrangements must include not only a source of financing but also a more effective method of delivery. The two are interconnected: So little money is available for international assistance today because the results are considered so unsatisfactory. The reputation of foreign aid is the worst in the United States. Countries that spend a larger portion of their GNP on aid also have better results to show.

Aid is needed for a great variety of purposes. We may distinguish between two broad categories: providing public goods on a global scale and fostering economic, social, and political progress in individual countries.

The first category includes environmental, educational, and health issues. The fight against infectious diseases, for example, cannot be confined to particular countries.

The second category refers, first and foremost, to the promotion of better government. It includes not only an efficient and honest central and local administration and an independent and reliable judiciary but also the rule of law and an appropriate relationship between the public and private spheres: a society that is not dominated by the state, a private sector that is not in cahoots with the government, and a civil society whose voice is heard. What is appropriate is bound to vary from country to country; Western democracy is not the only possible model. Yet there are some universal principles of liberty and human rights, including the freedom of speech and association and the treatment of minorities and minority opinions, that should be respected. To emphasize that there is no single blueprint that is appropriate in all cases, I speak of an open society as the objective.

Open society can be taken as a very broad expression of

democracy that also includes economic progress and the reduction of poverty. Making the promotion of open society the goal differs from the internationally endorsed goal of poverty reduction in emphasizing the importance of the political arrangements prevailing in individual countries. The UN, being an association of sovereign states, had to shy away from this issue, but the fact is that poverty and misery are usually associated with bad governments. Admittedly, it is difficult to interfere in the internal affairs of sovereign countries, but it is important to face up to the problem.

There are some things that can and should be done by imposing international rules. There is plenty of room for expanding and strengthening international treaties. The Kyoto treaty or an improved version of it, the treaty on landmines, and that on the control of trade in small arms are highly desirable. The International Criminal Court ought to be brought into existence. But international treaties are hard to reach and even more difficult to enforce. The attitude of the United States is currently the major obstacle.

Imposing economic sanctions has limited use and can easily become counterproductive. Trade embargoes are often broken, and those who engage in smuggling are usually in cahoots with the regime the sanctions are supposed to punish. The net effect is to punish the people but provide economic sustenance to the regime. That is how sanctions worked in Iraq and Yugoslavia. Unilateral sanctions like those imposed by the United States on Cuba are even less effective. Recently there has been a move toward so-called smart sanctions: travel restrictions and financial measures aimed at people associated with the regime. These hold greater promise.

The most promising approach is to offer positive induce-ments for voluntary compliance—in short, foreign aid. It may not apply to hardened cases like Iraq and the former Yugoslavia, but it would encourage and empower govern-ments that are genuinely interested in improving social conditions. In the case of repressive regimes, foreign aid ought to be confined to nongovernmental channels.

Both the IMF and the World Bank are deeply engaged in providing technical and financial assistance to countries that are ill prepared to compete in a global economy. These countries comprise what used to be called the sec-ond and the third worlds—the formerly communist coun-tries and the less-developed countries—as well as a number of countries that have developed as closed economies and have not yet adjusted to free trade and the free movement of capital; this includes much of Asia and Latin America and practically all of Africa. Together, they constitute the majority of the world's population.

Structural adjustments are needed in many institutions, ranging from the judiciary to healthcare and education, and in many sectors of the economy, ranging from banking to agriculture and energy. Although the problems vary from country to country, the IFIs have shown a tendency to apply a common approach. The approach is largely dictated by the nature of the relationship between the IFIs and the recipient countries. Most of the assistance has taken the form of loans to governments, with an element of technical assistance.

The IMF and the World Bank play somewhat different institutional roles. The World Bank has a large staff and tends to be more hands-on in designing and implementing sectoral loans. The IMF has a smaller staff focused on macroeconomic issues. It relies on the recipient governments to implement a plan specified in a letter of intent. If a government fails to meet the specified conditions, the IMF stops disbursing funds.

Because the IFIs control the funds, they act as the arbiters of what kind of economic reforms they will support and on what conditions. The IFIs have developed a more or less standardized approach to economic reform: The IMF has a prevailing doctrine and the World Bank offers a standard menu from which the recipients can choose.

This approach has produced very mixed results. For instance, a World Bank evaluation of 10 African programs lists two successes, two outright failures, and the rest somewhere in between.* Evaluations from other parts of the world are not very different.

The most ambitious undertaking entrusted to the IFIs—assisting the countries of the former Soviet empire in making the transition to a market economy—has fallen far short of expectations. Some of the former satellites have muddled through, but Russia has only recently begun to show signs of economic recovery with market reforms taking hold.

In my view, the task should never have been entrusted to the IFIs. The IMF makes borrowing governments sign letters of intent and suspends disbursements if the bor-

*Aid and Reform in Africa: Lessons from Ten Case Studies, edited by Shantayanan Devarajan, David Dollar, and Torgny Holmgren (Washington, D.C.: The International Bank for Reconstruction and Development/The World Bank, April 2001).

rowers fail to meet the conditions.* When governments break down, as happened in most of the formerly communist countries, they are not in a position to carry out their intent. A different, more intrusive approach was needed, and at that time it would have been welcomed by the Soviet Union and the successor states. The right policy would have been for the West to come to their aid as the United States did in postwar Europe with the Marshall Plan. But the idea was not even considered. When I proposed it at an East-West conference in Potsdam in 1989, I was literally laughed at by the audience, led by the Deputy Foreign Secretary of the Thatcher government.† The Western democracies did not want to take the responsibility, nor did they want to foot the bill out of their own budgets. That is why they assigned the task to the IMF and the World Bank.

When the IMF got the assignment, I proposed that it should use a more purposeful and intrusive way of delivering its support.** I proposed that a $10 billion IMF program for Russia be earmarked for the payment of pensions

---

*The conditions are formalized in Memoranda of Understanding.
†My proposal was "greeted with amusement" according to the *Frankfurter Allgemeine Zeitung.*
**George Soros, "A Cold-Cash Winter Proposal for Russia," *The Wall Street Journal*, November 11, 1992, page A10.

---

and unemployment benefits and that its disbursement be organized and supervised by the IMF. The same money that was given to the government for balance of payments and budgetary support could have also been used to provide a social safety net, but instead of disappearing in government coffers the money would have been broadly distributed and people in Russia would have seen visible evidence of international assistance. The scheme would have encouraged the restructuring of industry by generating consumer demand, and it would have provided some measure of social protection for those who were displaced by such restructuring.

Since the scheme was not even considered, I set out to demonstrate that it was feasible. I established the International Science Foundation with $100 million and distributed less than $20 million to some 35,000 leading scientists in the former Soviet Union according to very transparent criteria of excellence. The scientists did in fact receive $500 each on which they could live for a year.* It was perhaps the only case in which people received help in a tangible form and they—and society at large—have never forgotten it. This demonstrated on a small scale what could have been done on a larger scale. Imagine if all the

*It was a period of hyperinflation.

pensioners had received their pensions and the unemployed had been given unemployment benefits: I am convinced that history would have taken a different course. Consider the difference that the Marshall Plan made in postwar Europe, not only in fostering economic reconstruction but in generating lasting ties of goodwill. As it is, a historic opportunity was lost. Standards of living in the former Soviet Union dropped precipitously, and a rapacious and violent business culture took hold.*

The international community has not done much better in the Balkans. Billions were spent in Bosnia with very little to show for it. There was inadequate coordination among donors, and most of the aid went through governmental channels.† With so many donors competing to pass through the same gates, the gatekeepers could divert the funds to their own purposes.

There are lessons to be learned from these failures. The shortcomings of international assistance have been exten-

---

*Both absolute and relative poverty increased sharply in the transition countries, according to World Bank data. See *World Development Report 2000/2001* (Washington, DC: World Bank 2000), Table 1.2.
†I proposed setting up a fund to finance SMEs in partnership with the World Bank, but the Bosnian government insisted on controlling the fund. The World Bank had to comply with the requirements of the Bosnian government, but I did not: The fund never came into existence.

sively studied, and a new paradigm is emerging. It is recognized that the countries themselves must take charge of their development programs, and governments must consult with their citizens in preparing them. The World Bank has pioneered Comprehensive Development Frameworks (CDF), and the IMF, together with the Bank, requires a Poverty Reduction Strategy Paper (PRSP) in connection with concessional loans and debt forgiveness for Highly Indebted Poor Countries (HIPC). These initiatives are in their infancy, but they show promise and deserve to be encouraged.*

Although I am in sympathy with the emerging new paradigm, I believe there are other lessons to be learned. One of them is that the IFIs are ill suited to deal with the problem of bad governments. They are obliged by their charters to go through governmental channels. This makes them bureaucratic, and bureaucrats are risk averse. One of the advantages of letters of intent is that the IMF cannot be blamed if the intent is not carried out. Going outside governmental channels entails a much higher level of responsibility. Bureaucracies are justified in avoiding or deflecting risk; they can be second-guessed by a whole range of kibitzers. International bureaucracies are partic-

*I have used the acronyms in common use in official circles to indicate the bureaucratic nature of the enterprise.

ularly vulnerable because they have to serve a multitude of masters. Both the U.S. Congress and the European Parliament have shown a tendency to micromanage foreign aid. In recent years, the U.S. Congress has extended micromanagement to the activities of multilateral institutions like the UN and the IFIs.

Systemic reform is a high-risk enterprise. The risks are even greater than in private enterprise, and there is no single bottom line by which success can be judged. Social change is a nonlinear, reflexive process. What is the right policy at one moment of time may no longer be appropriate at the next. This means that the outcome cannot be predicted in advance. Systemic reform is a hit-or-miss affair, as uncertain as the behavior of financial markets.*

The IFIs have an important role to play. They can play it best when they deal with a reform-minded government that they can assist. The new paradigm may help the IFIs to perform better. But there is a pressing need to go beyond governmental channels. There are certain functions that only governments can fulfill, and one of the best uses of foreign aid is to increase the capacity of govern-

*William Easterly, *The Elusive Quest for Growth: Economists' Adventures and Misadventures in the Tropics* (Boston: MIT Press, 2001) gives an insightful account of the pitfalls of international assistance and the unpredictability of outcomes.

ments. But governments are not the most efficient economic agents; there is something wrong with international assistance if it serves to increase the role that governments play in the economy.

When the Soviet system collapsed the West failed to provide adequate support to governments to fill the role they have to play in a market economy, and instead of a transition there was a collapse. We discovered the hard way that the collapse of a closed society does not automatically lead to the creation of an open society, and a nonfunctioning state can be as much of a threat to liberty and prosperity as a repressive one.*

By the same token, international assistance given to repressive or corrupt regimes can go to reinforce those regimes. In some cases, foreign aid becomes the main source of support for those regimes. That is apt to happen when the aid is guided by geopolitical considerations. It happened often during the Cold War and is likely to happen again as the United States wages war on terrorism.

The use of nongovernmental channels becomes particularly important in the absence of a reform-minded gov-

*Stephen Holmes, "What Russia Teaches Us Now: How Weak States Threaten Freedom," *The American Prospect* (July-August 1997): 30–39.

do we want to support governments – or not confusing

still seems self contradictory

why But ?

ernment. International assistance can then foster an open society by providing a precious counterweight to a domineering and inefficient government. But support of the private sector and civil society is also essential where there is a reform-minded government. A democratic government should encourage the use of nongovernmental channels.

It can be seen that international assistance is a complicated business. There is no single formula to fit all cases. Instead of a bureaucratic approach we should take an entrepreneurial one. But social entrepreneurship is even more difficult than making money, as I have learned from personal experience. In making money there is a simple criterion of success: the bottom line. All the various items that enter into the account serve a single goal: profit. In serving the public good the situation is reversed. Instead of a single line, the social consequences of an undertaking show up in a variety of lines, and the various lines cannot be readily aggregated. The GNP is often used as a proxy, but that can be very misleading because different people *yes . also in the US* are affected differently and there are many unintended consequences. Judged by the standards applied in business, international assistance is bound to be inefficient. One of the reasons foreign aid has such a bad reputation in the United States is that it is judged by the wrong standard.

Social entrepreneurship ought to play a larger role in international assistance. It should not replace intergovernmental programs but be additional to them. There are many successful social initiatives, but they lack sufficient resources. The amounts available for international assistance are far from sufficient and have been falling since 1990, according to the OECD. In November 2001, British Chancellor of the Exchequer Gordon Brown called for $50 billion additional foreign aid annually from the rich countries of the world, but his proposal did not appear to get serious consideration at the subsequent meeting of the IFIs in Ottawa. To mobilize additional resources, the public must be convinced that the money will be well spent. That requires explaining the difficulties inherent in foreign aid and finding better ways to administer it.

The Tobin Tax

Several innovative sources of financing for foreign aid have been suggested, but none will be adopted unless public opinion demands it. One of the more popular proposals was put forth by the Nobel Prize-winning economist James Tobin, for a tax on currency transactions. There is a case to be made for such a tax, but it is somewhat different from the argument put forward by Professor Tobin. It is not at all clear that a "Tobin tax" would reduce volatility in currency markets—its stated purpose.

It is true that a "Tobin tax" would discourage currency speculation, but it would also reduce the liquidity of the marketplace so that chunky transactions, such as the acquisition of large companies, would have a greater impact on exchange rates. This could be counterbalanced by the more frequent use of official reserves—for instance currency for large corporate transactions could be provided from official reserves—but that would involve a substantial change in how currency markets are managed, and there is no evidence that the authorities are willing to take on the additional responsibility.

The case for a Tobin-type tax is different. The globalization of financial markets has given financial capital an unfair advantage over other sources of taxation; a tax on financial transactions would redress the balance. Why should there be a Value Added Tax (VAT) on physical transactions, but no tax on financial transactions? On these grounds the tax ought to be extended to all financial markets, not only currency markets. There are serious problems of implementation, but these could be resolved. How could derivatives and synthetic instruments be taxed?

This looks like a thorny problem, but in fact it is easily solved. There is a measure that shows the equivalent of a derivative in terms of the underlying security, called Delta.* The tax could be levied on the Delta of derivatives at the time of the transaction. The problems connected with the collection of the tax are more serious. Collection has to be worldwide, including tax havens. How could it be enforced? The collecting country has to be given a share of the proceeds. How big a share should that be? All these problems could serve as an excuse for not introducing a financial transaction tax. Even if they were overcome the question of how to spend the money effectively would remain.

As antiglobalization protests have demonstrated, it is easier to organize people against something than for something. To mobilize public opinion in favor of increased international assistance, the proposal must show not only how the money will be raised but also how it will be spent.

*Delta is the change in the value of an option that corresponds to the change in the value of the underlying security. For instance, a one-month call option on $1 million dollar/yen at a strike price of yen 125 when the spot price is yen 122 is equivalent to an outright position of $181,100 dollar/yen.

The SDR Proposal

Special Drawing Rights

I have such a proposal: It involves issues of SDRs that the rich countries would donate for the purpose of providing international assistance. It is an initiative that could make a substantial amount of money available almost immediately, to finance the provision of public goods on a global scale as well as to foster economic, social, and political progress in individual countries; it is an initiative that could point the way to a large, continuous, and predictable flow of financing for development indefinitely.*

SDRs are international reserve assets issued by the IMF to its members and convertible into other currencies. Less-developed countries would add their SDRs to their monetary reserves; richer countries (as defined in the IMF "transaction plan") would donate their allocations according to certain rules. Less-developed countries would benefit both directly through the addition to their monetary reserves and indirectly from the provision of public goods on a global scale.

There is widespread agreement that the amount of money available for international assistance has to be significantly

*See box on pages 76–77 for a description of SDRs.

increased. The Zedillo Report, prepared for the Monterrey Conference on Financing Development, estimates that meeting the 2015 UN development targets may require an extra $50 billion per year, and seriously addressing the need for public goods another $20 billion.* The British Chancellor of the Exchequer, Gordon Brown, called for an annual increase of $50 billion.

The proposal to use SDRs for international assistance would be implemented in two stages. In the first stage, a special 21.43 billion SDR issue (approximately $27 billion) already authorized by the IMF in 1997 and currently awaiting ratification by the U.S. Congress, would be approved by Congress with the proviso that the richer countries donate their allocations in accordance with certain rules. Since the richer countries will get most of the SDR allocation even under the amended formula of the 1997 decision, nearly $18 billion could be made immediately available for international assistance.† This would be a practical test of the idea. If successful, the initial issue would be followed by regular annual allocations of SDRs, and the amounts could be scaled up. Clearly, the scheme

*The report of the United Nations Secretary General's High Level Panel on Financing for Development, chaired by former Mexican President Ernesto Zedillo. See www.un.org/esa/ffd/a55-1000.

†Assuming that all 38 members currently included in the "transaction plan" contributed their SDR allocations. See *Financing IMF Transactions, Quarterly Report*

the money – as I understand this – would be a tax on money on money exchange/speculation transactions – NOT from why normal tax base.

proposed here could go a long way toward meeting generally agreed development targets.

Using SDRs to fund international assistance would not only increase the total amount available for international assistance; it would also ensure that all developed countries contribute equitably because the quota-based distributions of SDR allocations are roughly proportional to the economic strength of member countries. Any common effort suffers from the so-called freerider problem: The community as a whole is better off if the effort succeeds, but each member of the community is better off by not contributing. Use of the SDR mechanism cures the freerider problem. Most important, the scheme proposed here would correct many of the shortcomings of foreign aid, especially as it is currently administered by governmental aid agencies. These advantages ought to be preserved whether or not the SDR mechanism is adopted.

(Washington, DC: International Monetary Fund, June 1, 2001–August 31, 2001).

Because of the way the allocation formula was constructed, certain anomalies occur in the distribution of the special SDR allocation. For example, the United Kingdom will get a very small allotment. Some arrangement would have to be made to ensure that the United Kingdom contributes its fair share. These anomalies would disappear in regular SDR allocations, which are based on countries' quota shares, which in turn roughly reflect countries' relative economic strength.

EXPLANATION OF THE SDR

The International Monetary Fund has the authority under its Articles of Agreement to issue Special Drawing Rights (SDRs). SDRs, created in 1969, are international reserve assets that serve as a unit of account and as means of payment among Fund members, the Fund itself, and prescribed "other holders." Other holders must be approved by the IMF executive board by an 85 percent majority. The SDRs constitute part of a country's official foreign exchange reserves. A number of international agencies and development banks use the SDR as a unit of account. Members and prescribed holders may buy and sell SDRs for foreign exchange; borrow, lend, or pledge SDRs; use SDRs in swaps and forward operations; use them in settlement of financial obligations; and use or receive SDRs in donations.

The value of the SDR is determined by a basket of the four major currencies: the U.S. dollar, the euro, the yen, and the pound sterling. On January 1, 2002, the value was SDR1 = US $1.25673. IMF members can use the SDR to purchase currencies from other members at the current exchange rate, which is adjusted daily. The IMF will help "other holders" of SDRs arrange purchases of currencies.

The SDR is an interest-bearing instrument. Members receive the SDR interest rate on their holdings and pay the SDR interest rate on their allocations. The SDR interest rate (paid by members drawing down their original allocations to purchase currencies from other members, and earned by members whose SDR holdings increase as a result of such transactions) is based on a weighted average of representative short-term debt of the countries whose currencies constitute the SDR basket (France, Germany, Japan, the United Kingdom, and the United States) and is adjusted weekly. On January 1, 2002, the SDR interest rate was 2.23 percent. Interest is paid quarterly.

SDRs are created through a process of allocation and distribution to IMF members. The most recent SDR allocation was made in 1981, bringing cumulative allocations to SDR 21.4 billion. SDR allocations must be approved by an 85 percent "supermajority" of total voting power in the IMF and are distributed to the individual member countries according to quota share. The IMF can cancel SDRs but has not done so.

In 1997, the IMF members agreed to amend the IMF Articles to allow a single special "equity" allocation of SDRs that would channel a bigger share to the former Soviet republics and other transition countries as well as poorer member countries than would result from the standard quota-based distribution.

An amendment of the Articles also requires an 85 percent majority for ratification. As of December 2001, members representing 72.7 percent of the vote had ratified the Fourth Amendment. Ratification by the United States, which has 17.13 percent of the total vote, is necessary to put it over the top. This would require approval of the U.S. Congress. Ratification of the amendment would trigger an immediate new allocation of SDR 21.433 billion, doubling the total outstanding and significantly boosting the foreign exchange reserves of transition and poorer countries, although the wealthier members would still get almost two-thirds of the total allocation under the modified formula.

IMF = international monetary fund

who are these "wealthier countries — ? Is China one of them?

As mentioned before, the contribution of individual countries to international assistance is highly uneven; the United States is the laggard, with only one-tenth of 1 percent of its GDP devoted to foreign aid. The proposed special issue amounts to roughly 0.1 percent of the global GDP, and subsequently the size of the issues could be scaled up. Since the SDR donations are designed to be additional to the present level of foreign aid, the use of SDRs should ensure a greater volume of international assistance and a more equitable distribution of the cost. Even more important is the mechanism that would be used to distribute the aid. A new approach to financing would be accompanied by a new approach to managing international assistance. I propose creating a kind of market in which programs compete for donors' funds. This is how it would work.

Under the proposed plan, an international board operating under the aegis of the IMF but independent of it would be set up to decide which programs are eligible for SDR donations.* The board's members would be eminent persons appointed for fixed terms and not under direct instruction from their governments. A separate audit commission would arrange for independent monitoring and evaluation. The board would propose a strategy in its

---

*The IMF Articles require that holders of SDRs other than the IMF itself and its member governments have to be "prescribed," that is, approved, by the IMF executive board with an 85 percent majority. Other holders have to be "official

annual report, but it would have no authority over the spending of funds. It would merely prepare a menu from which the donors would be free to choose, creating a marketlike interplay between donors and programs, supply and demand. The quality of the programs would be ensured by the board, and the quality of the donors' choices would be open to public scrutiny.

It may not be appreciated how important it is that the international board consist of eminent persons selected on the basis of publicly stated professional qualifications and not the usual government appointees. In the case of the UN-sponsored trust fund to fight HIV/AIDS, tuberculosis, and malaria currently in formation, all the major donors want to be represented on the board, and it is only with difficulty that the size of the board has been whittled down to 18; seven of the board seats are still reserved for the G7 countries. The Secretary General of the UN is not in a good position to exert pressure on member countries because he is their servant; a board of eminent persons would be much better situated.

The menu would include trust funds for the provision of public goods on a global scale as well as matching funds

---

entities." The proposal here is that the executive board should delegate the responsibility of determining eligibility to receive donated SDRs to an independent board, although technically it would retain legal authority.

other sources of funds

for a variety of social initiatives. For the first SDR issue the list of eligible programs would be confined to three or four specific priority areas such as public health, education, information (the digital divide), and judicial reform.* Government-sponsored poverty reduction programs would be excluded; they would be left to the IFIs. This would help to make the test more successful. The specific program areas could be dealt with by sub-boards whose members would have the necessary professional qualifications. There would be also a better delineation of responsibilities and less room for institutional rivalry. In the case of public health, the board of the newly formed trust fund to fight infectious diseases could act as the sub-board *provided* the donors agreed to the selection process proposed here.

If the implementation of the first SDR issue is successful and SDRs are issued annually, the range of eligible programs would be expanded. Government-sponsored poverty reduction programs could also qualify, but only

*I propose to include judicial reform because IFIs are not allowed to pay supplemental salaries to judges and governmental employees. That is often the stumbling block to judicial reforms and anticorruption programs. For instance, Georgia, one of the most corrupt countries of the world, appointed qualified judges selected by competitive examination by promising decent salaries but subsequently was unable to deliver on its promise, and the World Bank supported reform effort failed. Programs eligible under this scheme would not be subject to that constraint.

up to a certain limit in order to leave funds for nongovernmental channels. By that time the new paradigm currently being formulated by the IFIs (CDF and PRSP) will have been elaborated. Some limits, however, would have to be placed on the amount of SDRs that can be committed to government-sponsored programs; otherwise, they are liable to absorb all the available funds. Governments prefer intergovernmental channels. It is important that other initiatives should not be starved of funds because, as I stressed previously, there is no single formula to fit all cases.* I shall give some practical examples of the kind of programs that ought to qualify for support.

My foundation got involved in a program for treating tuberculosis (TB) in Russian prisons in 1997. Our goal was to improve prison conditions, and we sought to gain the cooperation of the prison authorities by treating a disease that affected prisoners and prison guards alike. We applied an up-to-date method of treatment recommended by the World Health Organization (WHO) called DOTS —directly observed treatment–short course—thinking that with a $15 million grant we could make a major impact. Soon we discovered that an overwhelming number of prisoners were infected with multi-drug-resistant strains

*Cf. Easterly, *The Elusive Quest for Growth*, 113.

of tuberculosis (MDR-TB). Since MDR-TB was impervious to DOTS treatment, sticking to DOTS could have actually increased the incidence of MDR-TB. MDR-TB constitutes a costly global threat—an epidemic in the jail on Rikers Island and other parts of New York City in the early 1990s cost approximately $1 billion to control. Obviously, we had run into a problem in Russia that far exceeded our financial capacity, as curing MDR-TB at that time would have cost $15,000 per patient. We mobilized the best experts in the field and commissioned Partners in Health in Boston to prepare a study on the global impact of MDR-TB. One of the outcomes was the reduction of the cost of treating MDR-TB to as little as $300 per patient. As a next step, we then asked Partners in Health to develop a business plan for dealing with TB on a global scale. Together with STOP-TB—a partnership of 190 collaborating organizations including the WHO, the World Bank, governments of the 22 most directly affected countries, and representatives of the NGO community and private sector—they produced a "Global Plan to Stop TB." The plan was unveiled at the World Bank in Washington in October 2001. It calls for spending $9.3 billion over five years: $4.8 billion would come from the budgets of the affected and donor countries, leaving a financing gap of $4.5 billion. That gap could be filled by the donation of SDRs. The "Global Plan to Stop TB" could also be helpful in pointing the way for the newly formed UN-sponsored Global Fund to Fight AIDS, TB, and Malaria.

We should "cure" over-births" at the same time.

As regards creating a marketlike interaction between donors and programs, my foundation network has participated in preparing a Global Exchange for Social Investment, which will be introduced at the World Economic Forum meeting in February 2002. Bain & Company has acted as principal consultant on a pro bono basis. They have developed a certification process to designate authorized intermediaries who, in turn, submit a list of projects for which they are willing to take moral or administrative responsibility. Corporate donors, foundations, and philanthropically minded individuals are invited to go shopping from the list. This is a practical private sector test of the SDR donation scheme I am proposing. If successful, the Global Exchange for Social Investment could be included in the list that qualifies for matching funds from SDR donations.

Microlending would constitute an important element in social entrepreneurship. There is ample evidence to show that it can work. The difficulty is in scaling it up. Successful microlending operations are largely self-sustaining, but they cannot grow out of retained earnings or raise capital in the financial markets. To turn microlending into a significant factor in economic and political progress, ways have to be found to attract additional capital. This would require general support for the industry as well as capital for individual ventures. Industry support would include developing management software and making it available as a public good, training managers, and establishing a rating agency and a loan guarantee scheme. The rating agency would help to attract philanthropically minded equity investors who would be willing to accept below-market returns or no return at all; the loan guarantee scheme would enable qualified microlending institutions to issue commercial paper. (The World Bank's callable capital could also be used for guarantees, giving the paper AAA rating.)*

Another important element would be stipends for educational purposes along the lines developed by Bolsa-Escola, the Brazilian scheme that pays subsidies to poorer families provided their children attend school regularly. Combining educational stipends with healthcare and microlending could move large segments of the population out of poverty.

*The importance of a rating agency is illustrated by the recent problems of the Grameen Bank in Bangladesh, reported in *The Wall Street Journal*, November 27, 2001, page 1.

The SDR donation mechanism could be particularly useful in connection with regional or national donor conferences. The Balkans provide an excellent example. There was general agreement on the need for a coordinated regional approach. This led to the establishment of the Stability Pact for South Eastern Europe, but the Pact remained an empty shell because the donors retained control of the amounts pledged and followed their own agendas. If the Stability Pact had been designated as a potential recipient of SDR donations, the projects collected and approved by the so-called Working Tables of the pact might have received adequate funding, and international assistance could have been more successful.

Afghanistan is another case in point. If donor countries retain control over the spending of their donations, failure is almost guaranteed. A more coordinated approach is needed. Aid should be delivered at the community level, and instead of a large number of aid agencies running around in an uncoordinated manner, a lead agency has to be put in charge. In this case the UNDP is well situated. Together with other UN agencies, it has had several thousand Afghan employees on the ground during the conflict, and their numbers could be rapidly increased by recruiting among the diaspora. Giving control of the purse strings to an international agency like the UNDP could

UNDP = United Nations Development Program.

avoid repeating the mistakes of the past. Local warlords could stick to their territories instead of fighting for control of Kabul as they have done previously. Of course, UNDP personnel in charge of money would have to be protected by a UN peacekeeping force, but the newly formed government could not object because that is the only way that recovery aid would be made available. After a period of consolidation, the UNDP would withdraw and a newly elected government would take over the local infrastructure that has been established.* Admittedly, all this could be done without SDRs, but the SDR scheme, if it were available, would facilitate the pooling and joint management of donor resources.

There is a strong case to be made for annual SDR allocations quite apart from the donation scheme. As a consequence of globalization, international trade has been growing at roughly double the rate of global GDP. To avoid balance of payments disruptions, countries must maintain a prudent ratio of reserves to imports. Typically, reserves equal to three months' imports are regarded as the absolute minimum. It follows that poor countries have to set aside part of their export earnings to build up their reserves. The SDR allocations would ease this burden.

*Soros, "Assembling Afghanistan," *Washington Post*, December 3, 2001, page A21.

The burden has become heavier since the emerging market crisis of 1997–1999 because of the reverse flow of capital from emerging markets.

The developed countries have no use for SDR allocations because their monetary reserves are adequate—in the case of Eurozone countries even redundant*—and if they ran a payment deficit they could always borrow. That is why it has been so difficult to forge a consensus in favor of issuing SDRs. But if the developed countries found a use for SDRs by donating them, the case for issuing SDRs would be greatly strengthened.

Central banks have been traditionally opposed to SDR allocations because they infringe on their monopoly of the money supply. Their mantra has been that SDRs are inflationary. But the prospects for inflation in the near term are low. Indeed, there is a possibility that the steady decline in the cost of imported goods could lead to global deflation. As the case of Japan shows, there are no readily available remedies against deflation. An annual issue of SDRs, the bulk of which is actually spent on international assistance, could turn out to be a useful monetary tool.

I'm not sure I understand this .

*The combined foreign exchange reserves of the European Central Bank and national central banks totaled EUR 393 billion in October 2001.

Legal Consideration

The regular issuance of SDRs is already provided for in the IMF's Articles of Agreement. The rules also specifically stipulate that SDRs may be donated. Linking SDRs and aid has been discussed off and on, including during the 1980s debt crisis. In 1986, the Interim Committee, the IMF's ministerial advisory body, rejected such a link, stating that, "The Committee stressed the monetary character of the SDR, which should not be a means of transferring resources, and recommended that the Executive Board study possible improvements in the monetary character of the SDR that would increase its attraction and usefulness as a component of monetary reserves."* But the 1997 IMF decision on a one-time allocation with a special distribution formula that would result in transition and emerging market countries getting a bigger share broke with the principle affirmed in 1986. The clear intent of this decision was to transfer resources—in this case, monetary reserves.

In the most recent discussion of the subject, the IMF reaffirmed that under its Articles "SDRs can be allocated only on the basis of a finding of long-term global need or, upon

*IMF Annual Report 1986 (Washington, DC: International Monetary Fund, 1986), 111.

This has to be 4th amendment to the IMF Articles

adoption of the Fourth Amendment, through a one-time special allocation." In response to my proposal it was acknowledged that "there is nothing to prevent countries from voluntarily agreeing to transfer SDRs to other countries or prescribed holders for reasons of their own choosing . . . . The mechanics of the Soros proposal are similar to earlier proposals involving a post-allocation redistribution of SDRs through quasi-independent trust funds."* Since there is a long-term need to supplement reserves by issuing SDRs quite independently of the donation scheme, my proposal clearly meets legal requirements. The donation scheme makes the case for issuing SDRs even stronger. Whether to use SDRs for international assistance is therefore clearly a political decision. I believe the time is ripe for it.

Whether SDR donations should be treated as a budget item is a vexing question. A case can be made for both alternatives. In principle, the allocation of SDRs is a book-keeping item, but when the SDRs are donated that is a real expenditure. That is the case for including it in the budget. But the allocation of SDRs goes to strengthen the monetary reserves—in the case of the United States,

---

*"SDR Allocation in the Eighth Basic Period—Basic Consideration," IMF Staff Report (Washington, DC: International Monetary Fund, November 16, 2001), box 3, page 13.

the Exchange Stabilization Fund. If an equivalent amount is then withdrawn and spent, the monetary reserves remain unaffected except for the interest obligations vis-à-vis the Fund. Central banks, or in the U.S. case, the Treasury, do not normally seek appropriations to cover changes in their foreign exchange reserves including interest earned or lost—that is the case for making the donations outside the budget. Putting SDR donations through the budget process could create difficulties, particularly in EU countries that are up against the limits imposed by the Maastricht Treaty and the Stability Pact. Avoiding the budget process altogether would run into the strenuous opposition of the monetary authorities, and rightly so because it would be a breach of budget discipline.

Under its Articles, the IMF may cancel as well as create SDRs. It could be argued that donations of SDRs should be put through the budget process only when the SDRs are recalled, because it is only then that the donation has an impact on the balance sheet of the central bank, or in the case of the United States, the Exchange Stabilization Fund. In the end, it is up to each country to decide how to treat its SDR donations. The United States may decide to include it in the budget at the time the donation is made or not to include it; EU countries may use their excess monetary reserves for the purpose.

Merits of the Proposal

The SDR proposal would help poor countries in two ways: indirectly through the donations and directly through an addition to their monetary reserves. The addition is interest-free because as long as they hold on to their SDR allocations the interest income and expenditure cancel out each other. That is as close to a free lunch as possible; it is free as long as you don't eat it. The SDR scheme kills two birds with one stone, which makes it more efficient but also more difficult to explain.

SDR donations would be additional to and not a replacement for bilateral aid. The donations would be voluntarily deposited in an escrow account, and if they are not allocated, the interest would accumulate in that account and not accrue to the benefit of the donor country. This would ensure that the donations are actually spent. The scheme proposed here would prevent donor countries from using their SDR allocations to finance their bilateral aid programs.

most important feature

There is widespread opposition to the creation of new international institutions, particularly in the United States. Such institutions are perceived as bureaucratic and wasteful—and not without justification. Part of what makes them top-heavy and expensive to operate is that the member countries insist on exercising control and use the institutions for patronage. The scheme I am proposing would avoid that drawback. It would amount to a new international institution, but it would be radically different in character from the existing ones. The board would operate under the aegis of the IMF for legal reasons but in fact would be independent of it. It could be an extremely low overhead operation. The scheme would function more like an organized market: There would be public interaction between donors and programs reminiscent of the interaction between supply and demand. Both the performance of the programs and the allotment of SDRs would be open to public scrutiny. It may seem paradoxical that I should be advocating a kind of market in foreign aid after I had inveighed against the dangers of market fundamentalism, but I have never denied the merits of markets as a feedback mechanism.

For a foreign aid "market" to be successful, it is important to realize that it is bound to be less efficient than a normal market. As mentioned previously, there is no single criterion of success similar to the bottom line in business. There are some objectives that can be measured by quantitative indicators such as mortality or literacy, but it would be limiting and distorting to confine the objectives to those that have quantitative indicators. Success is harder to achieve in a social enterprise than in business, and it is even harder to measure. Once the point is accepted, failures will be better tolerated and successes more appreciated. That would make social entrepreneurship easier to practice and would attract more talent.

In the Introduction, I identified five factors that render international assistance ineffectual. I believe the scheme I am proposing would mitigate those shortcomings.

- First, the ability of donors to use foreign aid to satisfy their own needs would be greatly reduced. Perceived national interests would of course continue to weigh heavily on the selection of projects, but there is nothing wrong with that.

- Second, a marketplace of projects would give both the donors and the project managers a sense of ownership and responsibility.

- Third, the stranglehold of intergovernmental dealings would be decisively broken. It is the great advantage of trust funds that they need not be channeled through governments.* Governments could no longer act as

---

*Trust funds could greatly enhance the usefulness of existing international insti-

very important
advantage

gatekeepers, and oppressive and corrupt regimes would
no longer have a license to misappropriate resources.
Instead of many donors competing to go through a single
entry point, namely the recipient government, there
would be many projects competing for donor support.
The gatekeeper problem would be resolved, at least in
theory.

- Fourth, donor coordination would be enhanced because
programs would have to be approved by a board to
qualify for SDR donations. With each country contributing according to its quota, the freerider problem
would be eliminated.

---

tutions. The UNDP in particular could play a valuable role. The UNDP, like
the World Bank, has a rather heavy infrastructure, with on-the-ground repre-
sentation in all the less-developed countries, but its official budget is much
smaller and its use is strictly circumscribed. Trust funds would give it more lee-
way. The UNDP would still need the approval of the host country, but trust
funds could concentrate on reform-minded governments and enhance their
capacity to absorb assistance. Trust funds would also be a channel for providing
resources directly to community groups in countries with nonreforming governments. This would be particularly valuable at times of revolutionary regime
change: It would remove a bottleneck that often stands in the way of success.
For instance, the UNDP in partnership with my foundation is paying supplemental stipends for qualified Yugoslav citizens returning from abroad. In many
countries, it would be necessary to pay qualified judges a supplemental salary at
least on a temporary basis to fight corruption. but at present no funds can be
found. The World Bank has a rule against paying the salaries of public servants.
The UNDP is well placed to fill this need.

- Fifth, it is to be hoped that the risks inherent in foreign aid would be better recognized and projects structured more like venture capital than a bureaucratic exercise. Even with the best will in the world, success is bound to vary considerably depending on timing, specific structural details, or sheer luck. A marketplace of projects cannot ensure the optimum allocation of resources, but it can take advantage of the main merit of markets by providing rapid, reliable feedback.

My optimistic expectations are based on real-life experience. The principles I have outlined here have been put into practice in my foundation network (although they were never spelled out so explicitly). The foundations have, in effect, functioned as trust funds, receiving their allotments from an international board. The results have largely conformed to the expectations stated here: Some have been great, others less so, but the positives outweigh the negatives and the negatives are rapidly identified and abandoned. Overall, I strongly believe the results are positive enough to justify applying the approach on a larger scale. Admittedly, a public enterprise cannot duplicate a private one, but it can benefit from its example.

The SDR proposal could be taken up at the UN's International Conference on Financing for Development, sched-

I wonder what did happen -

uled for Monterrey, Mexico, in March 2002, and be implemented at the next meeting of the IMF. It would not displace the other sources of financing discussed in the Zedillo Report. Those should also be considered, but I believe this proposal is superior in many respects. There are no problems of tax collection, the legal groundwork is already laid, and the scheme could be tested by a one-time allocation that only needs the approval of the U.S. Congress to become effective. Its main drawback is that it is complicated and difficult to understand. It serves more than one objective, and expert opinion on the use of SDRs as a monetary tool is bound to be divided. But where there is political will for more and better international assistance, there is a way to overcome all possible objections. In the post–September 11 atmosphere, with the Monterrey Conference in March 2002 and the G7 Summit focusing on Africa in June 2002, it should be possible to muster the political will.

The SDR donation scheme will not cure all of globalization's ills. Nor will the mechanism I have proposed for spending the SDRs avoid all the pitfalls of international assistance; it will only offer a better chance of making it more effective. That is all that one can expect in an imperfect society that holds itself open to improvement.

CHAPTER 3

Structural Reform: The Multilateral Development Banks

The World Bank was set up as a sister institution of the IMF. Its original mission was to provide long-term capital to countries whose infrastructure had been devastated by World War II at a time when little or no private capital was available. Gradually, it switched its focus to less-developed countries (LDCs). Regional development banks were set up on the model of the World Bank.

The World Bank's capital was contributed mainly in the form of guarantees from industrialized countries, against which the World Bank could borrow in capital markets with a AAA rating. This was an ingenious financial gimmick that conferred a benefit on poor countries at practically no cost to the rich ones. The guarantees have never been invoked.

The arrangement suffers from a significant drawback: It has locked the World Bank's lending into an intergovernmental straitjacket. The charter of the World Bank requires that its loans be guaranteed by the governments of the borrowing countries. The guarantees become instruments of control in the hands of the recipient governments. The loans often serve to reinforce corrupt or repressive regimes. The governments of the developed countries that dominate the board can also exercise a nefarious influence over the lending activities of the World Bank: They can push loans that benefit their export industries or veto loans that would create competition or otherwise hurt their interests.

In 1960, the International Development Association (IDA) was added to the World Bank to provide very low-interest, long-maturity loans to the poorest Bank member countries.* Subsequently, the World Bank set up another subsidiary, the International Finance Corporation (IFC), which can invest in and lend to the private sector. Further, it has established a Multilateral Investment Guarantee

---

*Currently, approximately 60 percent of IDA's lending is financed with donor contributions, the rest largely from re-flows and income generated by the Bank's loans. Annual lending by IDA is significant, averaging around $6–7 billion per year, but falls far short of the acute needs of the developing countries, and is only one-fourth to one-third of the amounts loaned through the Bank's non-concessional window.

Agency (MIGA), which is similarly directed at the private sector.

Originally the World Bank engaged mainly in large infrastructure projects, but as its focus shifted to developing countries, it has gradually reoriented itself toward creating human and social capital and alleviating poverty. Under the leadership of James Wolfensohn the changeover became more explicit and more pronounced. He introduced the idea of Comprehensive Development Frameworks (CDFs). Subsequently, debt forgiveness for HIPC has led to the PRSP, which is a joint Fund/Bank process. A new paradigm for international assistance is emerging that gives the recipients a greater sense of ownership, tries to reinforce those who make progress, and penalizes those who fail to meet targets. The IFIs are clearly trying to learn from their mistakes. Unfortunately, antiglobalizaiton activists and other critics are unwilling to give them the benefit of the doubt. These are early days. There is much confusion about the way the process is supposed to work; the roles of the IMF and the World Bank are far from clarified. The IFIs must be given time to elaborate the new paradigm.

Since James Wolfensohn took charge, the World Bank has undertaken much-needed social initiatives, from microlending to distance learning and fighting AIDS and other infectious diseases. It has begun to experiment with lending to subnational units and some NGOs, but its charter limits the scope of such efforts because loans must flow through the central governments. These activities could be carried out more effectively by giving grants and dealing directly with other elements of society besides the central government: the private sector, local government, and community groups. But the World Bank has only limited funds available for outright grants and technical assistance. These funds are derived mainly from the profits of the lending operations. IDA's Development Grant Facility is only $100 million. In my view the discretionary spending activities of the World Bank are much more beneficial, with fewer adverse side effects, than are its lending activities.

The Bush administration has recently proposed that the World Bank reduce its lending and increase its grantmaking activities. It calls for half of IDA's disbursements to be in the form of grants.

On the face of it, replacing loans by grants would be a step in the right direction. But as the president's proposal did not provide for additional funding, the actual effect could be to reduce the activities of the World Bank overall. That meshes with the recommendations of the Meltzer Commission, which was established by the U.S. Congress in November 1998 to recommend future U.S. policy toward the IFTIs.

In its final report, issued in March 2000, the Meltzer Commission criticizes the World Bank for being a bureaucratic organization with too large a staff and for engaging in lending activities that could be taken care of by the capital markets.* It recommends that the World Bank get out of its bread-and-butter lending business, return its guarantee capital to the industrialized countries, and reconstitute itself as a World Development Agency providing assistance to the worlds' poorest countries. The Meltzer Commission has a highly restrictive definition of eligibility: Countries with a per capita income in excess of $4,000 would be excluded, and starting at $2,500 official assistance would be limited. Callable capital would be reduced in line with the declining loan portfolio; the IFC would be merged into the World Development Agency and its $5.3 billion capital returned to shareholders; MIGA would be dissolved. It all amounts to a massive resource transfer from the World Bank to the rich countries. As mentioned before, the Meltzer Commission called for an

---

*The International Financial Institution Advisory Commission (The Meltzer Commission) Report, March 2000. See www.house.gov/jec/imf/ifiac.htm.

increase in grants to the poorest countries "if grants are used effectively." There is a danger, however, that the downsizing of existing activities would be implemented while the increase in grants would get bogged down in working out the details.

I agree with the Meltzer Report that the World Bank's mission and operating methods ought to be reconsidered. Its lending business is inefficient, no longer appropriate, and in some ways counterproductive because it reinforces the role of the central government in the recipient countries. But I cannot agree that the role of the proposed World Development Agency should be as restricted as the Meltzer Commission would have it. There is too much poverty remaining in countries like Brazil, which would be excluded under the Meltzer formula. These countries also suffer from the high cost of capital. Local enterprises, particularly the small and medium-sized ones, are penalized vis-à-vis multinationals. Therefore there is no justification for returning capital to the rich countries or canceling the callable capital of the World Bank. Rather, the callable capital of the World Bank ought to be put to more active use.

Contrary to the Meltzer Commission's recommendation, it would be premature to terminate the existing lending operations of the World Bank. So-called middle income countries like Brazil, and even Chile, have very uneven income distributions and great social needs. Capital markets are rather intolerant of government expenditures and unforgiving toward accumulated debt in periphery countries. The World Bank has an important niche to fill.

The methods of the World Bank's lending operations do need to be reformed to eliminate unintended adverse consequences. The World Bank has to be more attentive to internal political conditions in the borrowing countries. This is already happening. CDFs envisage consultations with civil society. Transparency and the fight against corruption now rank high among the Bank's priorities. But more must be done. Even though the Bank cannot lend without the recipient governments' guarantees, the Bank should be more aggressive in monitoring whether its loans are disbursed on the basis of merit and not political influence. The Bank should refuse to make loans to repressive and corrupt regimes. The standards embedded in U.S. law are excellent and ought to be followed by other members.*

*Under Section 701 of the International Financial Institutions Act, the U.S. Executive Directors of the IFIs are instructed to oppose any loan or other assistance to governments that engage in "a consistent pattern of gross violations of internationally recognized human rights, such as torture or cruel, inhumane or degrading treatment or punishment, prolonged detention without charges, or

One of the benefits of the lending operation is that it does provide the World Bank with some discretionary income. Converting it into a World Development Agency would make it much more dependent on the donor governments, and that would expose it to all the disadvantages from which bilateral aid agencies suffer. The management of the Bank ought to be made less rather than more dependent on the donor governments. The bane of international aid is that the interests of the donors too often take precedence over the needs of the recipients.

To make the Bank less dependent on the shareholder governments, directors ought to be appointed based on their personal and professional qualifications for fixed terms and be given more independence from the governments that appointed them—as in the case of the United States with the governors of the Federal Reserve. Among other things, directors should not be expected to try to steer bank project procurement to their own nationals. The Bank's public bidding system offers some protection now. Nevertheless, U.S. legislation requires that an officer of the Foreign Commercial Service be assigned to the office of the U.S. Executive Director of the World Bank and all

other flagrant denial to life, liberty, and the security of person." The law exempts from this requirement "assistance directed specifically to programs which serve the basic human needs of the citizens of such country."

the regional development banks to look out for U.S. business interests. Some Bank trust funds financed by individual member governments are tied to procurement from nationals of that donor country. Other member governments may be more subtle, but the development business is also big business. Untying procurement is not enough; international assistance needs to be protected against the interests of the donors.*

At the same time, steps must be taken to prevent the interests of the staff from dominating the agency. This could be accomplished by putting a time limit on employment—say, five years, renewable once, based on performance. Those are the same term limits that apply to the president of the World Bank. Performance should not be measured by the amount of loans disbursed. The World Bank has a large and competent staff—too large, according to the Meltzer Report—drawn from all over the world, including the developing world. The staff is familiar with local conditions and concerned with social issues. But it is human nature that they are reluctant to go home. Term limits could provide talent-short home countries with a welcome infusion of desperately needed expertise.

*The Dutch have recently untied their money, the United Kingdom is doing the same, and pressure is growing for others to follow suit.

The Meltzer Commission's calculation that the World Bank guarantee capital constitutes a subsidy on the part of the United States and the other industrialized countries is highly contrived. The guarantees have never been invoked because Bank management knows that the shareholder countries would not stand for it. In my view, the argument ought to be turned on its head. There is an urgent need for the provision of public goods, and the rich countries ought to pay for them. Wealth redistribution used to take place on a national scale until globalization rendered progressive taxation counterproductive; now it ought to be practiced on a global scale.

One way to implement this principle would be to use the guarantee capital of the World Bank more actively by the Bank engaging in riskier activities. For example, the World Bank could guarantee commercial paper issued by a "Microcredit Finance Corporation." This would be a great boon to the world because microcredit and SME financing have proven themselves effective in reducing poverty. Microcredit, however, cannot grow without being continuously fed from the outside because it operates around break-even level. If the World Bank provided successful operations with additional capital, microcredit and SME financing could become a significant force in economic and political development.

Attractive as the idea is, it is impractical in today's world. The finance ministries of the developed countries would raise an outcry if they were required to make good on their guarantees. They would not authorize the World Bank to use its guarantee capital in such a way, and even if the Bank did, they would resist replenishing the guarantees. Given their attitude, the AAA rating of the World Bank could come into question.

In my judgment, this is not the right time to embark on a major reform of the World Bank, because any restructuring is liable to result in a reduction of its resources. It would be better to implement the SDR scheme than to try to put the guarantee capital of the World Bank to more active use. The time to reform the World Bank would come *after* the SDR scheme has proven successful. By then the IFIs will have had time to make the new paradigm work, and the atmosphere will have become more propitious for constructive reforms.

CHAPTER 4

Financial Stability: The International Monetary Fund

The case for global financial markets is less clear-cut than that for international trade. There is a fundamental difference between financial markets and markets for physical goods and services. The latter deal with known quantities, the former with quantities that are not merely unknown but actually unknowable.

Markets do show a tendency toward equilibrium when they deal with known quantities, but financial markets are different. They discount the future, but the future they discount is contingent on how the financial markets discount it at present. Instead of a predictable outcome, the future is genuinely uncertain and is unlikely to correspond to expectations. The bias inherent in market expectations is one of the factors that shape the course of events. There is a two-way interaction between expectations and outcomes that I call "reflexivity." *This shows how advanced we are in certain ways (at 2006), but also how primitive. If we had one stable world currency some of this instability would go away.*

The idea that market prices are influenced by market sentiment is nothing new. But the idea that market prices can influence the so-called fundamentals is less well recognized. For instance, the boom in Internet and telecommunication stocks accelerated the pace at which innovations could be introduced and allowed startup companies to capture the market for the most advanced products. Inversely, the bust is bringing a slowdown in new product introductions and allows established companies such as the regional telephone operators to gobble up the newcomers. This changes the relationship between supply and demand for many products, with profoundly negative effects on earnings. The jury is out on the question *stock earning* of whether the acceleration of productivity that could be observed in the last few years is going to be reversed in the next few years. *Most people do not understand what productivity means.*

I contend that reflexivity provides a better conceptual framework for understanding how financial markets function than the concept of equilibrium. Equilibrium implies a determinate outcome, but in financial markets the outcome is genuinely indeterminate. It is characteristic of reflexive situations that there is a divergence between expectations and outcomes, and participants cannot base their decisions on knowledge. Their judgments are biased, and the participants' bias becomes a factor in determining the outcome. At times the bias is so insignificant that it can be ignored; we can then speak of equilibrium. At other times the gap between expectations and outcomes is wider; we must then speak of far-from-equilibrium situations. Reflexivity allows for vicious and virtuous circles that are initially self-reinforcing but eventually self-defeating.

Systems theory would predict this —
reflexivity means feedback: vicious — negative ,
virtuous — positive.
(I think)

It should be emphasized that the implications of reflexivity are not generally recognized. On the contrary, economic theory, in its endeavor to produce determinate results, has gone to great lengths to leave it out of account. Financial economics is built on the assumption of efficient markets and rational expectations. I contend that the theory of rational expectations is self-contradictory: In conditions of radical uncertainty it is irrational to base one's expectations on the assumption that prices are based on rational expectations. In practice, few people do so.

Important

Admittedly, some advanced theoretical studies, notably the second generation of theories about financial crises, have taken reflexive phenomena into account and have recognized the possibility of what they call "multiple equilibria." But the prevailing view continues to be based on a fundamentally flawed market fundamentalist interpretation of how financial markets operate. That view is now endangering the stability of global financial markets.

Instead of moving toward equilibrium, financial markets, left to their own devices, are liable to go to extremes and eventually break down. Therefore they cannot be left to their own devices; they must be supervised, and to some extent managed, by the monetary authorities. Whatever the theory, this fact has been recognized in practice. The history of financial markets has been punctuated by crises, and each crisis has led to an addition to the regulatory framework. That is how central banking and the regulation of financial markets have evolved over time. The monetary authorities in the advanced industrial countries are well developed, but the evolution of the international regulatory framework has not kept pace with the globalization of financial markets. This can be seen by looking at recent history. The last 20 years have been marked by financial crises: the great international debt crisis that started in Mexico in 1982 and spread to most heavily indebted countries; another Mexican crisis in 1994 that spread to Latin America through the so-called tequila effect; and the emerging market crisis of 1997 that started in Asia and spread around the world, triggering the Russian default and ending with the devaluation of the Brazilian real in January 1999.

It is a distinguishing feature of these crises that they afflicted the periphery of the international financial system. The countries at the center remained largely unaffected because when they were threatened the monetary authorities took the appropriate actions to prevent a collapse of the international financial system.* This has caused a tremendous disparity in the economic and financial performance of the center and periphery. While the periphery went from crisis to crisis, the center remained remarkably stable and prosperous.† Being in charge of the system has given the center a significant advantage.

The fact that global financial markets have created a very uneven playing field does not fit the market fundamentalist doctrine, which holds that markets ensure the optimum

---

*The crisis of 1997–1999 threatened to engulf the international financial markets in the aftermath of the Russian default in August 1998. The U.S. Federal Reserve arranged a rescue operation to prevent failure of Long Term Capital Management (LTCM) and lowered interest rates three times in quick succession in October and November.

†A paper presented by Michael Hutchinson and Ilan Neuberger of the University of California at Santa Cruz at the Dubrovnik Economic Conference in June 2001 concluded that currency and balance of payments crises reduced output over two to three years by about 5 to 8 percent cumulatively. *IMF Survey*, July 30, 2001, page 259.

allocation of resources. Indeed, under the influence of market fundamentalism the emerging market crisis of 1997–1999 was an exception to the general rule that every crisis is followed by a strengthening of regulations. There has been some tightening of financial market and banking regulations in individual countries, but the general tendency has been to give greater play to market forces and a lesser role to official intervention at the international level.

Nobody questions the severity of the 1997–1999 crisis and the damage it has done, but opinions differ about the causes of the crisis. The prevailing view is that the way the IMF was operating interfered with market discipline and encouraged an irrational boom in international lending and investing, which then led to a bust. There were other factors at play as well: Many of the afflicted countries had unsound banking systems and followed inappropriate macroeconomic policies. But a root cause was deemed to be the moral hazard created by past IMF interventions; it was claimed that they led lenders to believe that in an emergency the IMF could be counted on to bail them out by coming to the rescue of the countries that got into difficulties in meeting their obligations. Whether this was valid or not, it came to be believed that future crises could be avoided by eliminating the moral hazard.*

*Shortly after his swearing in, U.S. Secretary of Treasury O'Neill told an inter-

I do not disagree with this argument completely. The intervention of the financial authorities did introduce a moral hazard, and the moral hazard did contribute to an untenable boom in emerging markets. Where I disagree is in the consequences of eliminating the moral hazard. Market fundamentalists claim that if you remove the moral hazard, market discipline will do the rest. I contend that financial markets are inherently unstable and the playing field is inherently uneven; curing the moral hazard will cause new dislocations, but in the opposite direction, creating a shortage of capital in the emerging markets. I believe that the IMF needs to play a larger rather than a lesser role and that special steps need to be taken to reduce the disparity between center and periphery.

The argument is not easy to present because the problems are quite complex and, in part, highly technical. I shall first give a brief historical overview of how we got where we are, then analyze the situation that has arisen in the aftermath of the 1997–1999 emerging market crisis, and finally put forward some proposals for reforming the international financial system.

---

viewer that the failure to stop financial crises was a failure to let markets work. "It doesn't have anything to do with the failure of capitalism. It's to do with an absence of capitalism." Gerard Baker and Stephen Fidler, "US Signals More Hands-off Stance on Global Markets," *Financial Times* (London), February 15, 2001, page 1.

A CAPSULE HISTORY OF THE IMF

When it was established at Bretton Woods in July 1944, the IMF was designed for a world characterized by fixed exchange rates and capital controls. Its mission was to make the growth of international trade possible by establishing rules for managing exchange rates and international payments and by providing temporary financing for adjustments in the balance of payments.

Capital controls were gradually lifted, and the fixed exchange rate system broke down in 1971. The first oil crisis of 1973 created profound imbalances in trade, and it was left to the commercial banks to finance them. There was a tremendous expansion in sovereign lending, which led to a crisis in 1982. Preserving the international banking system became a priority. The IMF was the lead agency in putting together rescue packages that allowed debtor countries to service their debt. The central banks exerted pressure on the commercial banks to "voluntarily" extend the maturities of their loans and to put up some "new" money so that the debtors could pay the interest due. On the whole, the IMF was successful in carrying out its mission: Major defaults were avoided. This was the origin of what came to be seen as a moral hazard: In case of crisis the lenders could look to the IMF for rescue.

[handwritten margin notes:] When petroleum producers deposited their projects to invest in. the banks were needing excess earnings in world banks, were paying interest not in the position of having too much capital

[handwritten note at bottom:] because it allowed. irresponsible borrowing

Most of the burden of adjustment fell on the debtor countries. It is true that the lenders had to set up reserves for bad debts and eventually, after the crisis had passed and the banks could afford it, much of the debt was reorganized in the form of Brady bonds, which yielded less and had longer maturities than the debts for which they were exchanged.* The first Brady bonds were issued by Mexico in 1989. On balance, the damage to debtor countries was much greater than to the banks: South America lost a decade of growth.
could not develop a middle class.
Under the liberalizing, deregulating impetus of the Reagan administration in the United States and the Thatcher government in the United Kingdom, international financial markets continued to develop apace during the 1980s even while the international lending crisis continued to fester. A plethora of derivatives, synthetic products, and other new financial products were introduced, and the financial landscape changed out of all recognition. That is when globalization truly took shape.

In 1994, Mexico ran into trouble once again. It had borrowed increasing amounts to preserve an overvalued exchange rate, and the government overspent prior to the 1994 elections; when the currency peg broke, the burden

---

*Named after U.S. Treasury Secretary Nicholas Brady.

of debt became unsustainable. Once again, the IMF came to the rescue with a large assist from the U.S. Treasury. The holders of tesobonos—Mexican treasury bills denominated in pesos but indexed to the U.S. dollar—were paid off in full and, according to market fundamentalists, the moral hazard became more pronounced.

That was the background against which the emerging market crisis of 1997–1999 unfolded. The IMF was once again called upon to intervene in Thailand, Indonesia, and South Korea. But this time the programs did not work, and the contagion spread until it engulfed almost the entire periphery of the global financial system.

It can be argued that the IMF applied the wrong prescription in the Asian crisis. Its programs consisted of allowing currencies to float, raising interest rates to contain the currency decline, and reducing government expenditures to contain the budget deficit. In addition, a number of conditions were imposed, aimed mainly at the banking system but also addressing other structural defects such as the sectoral monopolies in Indonesia. The outcome was to aggravate the economic collapse. The prescription had been developed in dealing with excesses in the public sector, but in this case the excesses had occurred in the private sector.*

*The IMF's own assessment of fiscal policy in the Asia programs is critical. See

118

It must be asked, however, whether the IMF had much of a choice. In my view, the appropriate course of action would have been to introduce a moratorium followed by debt reorganization. If the immediate pressure of debt repayments had been relieved, currency depreciation could have been contained without raising interest rates to punitive levels. The effect on the domestic economies would have been far less devastating. I have to admit, however, that a moratorium could have damaged the international financial system and spread the contagion. Since the primary mission of the IMF is to preserve the financial system, it could not take any chances. As it is, South Korea came close to a moratorium in December 1997, but the central banks intervened by leaning on the commercial banks to reschedule their loans on a "voluntary" basis. The arrangement was reminiscent of 1982, and it sent shudders through the financial markets. The contagion spread to Russia, and when Russia eventually defaulted in

---

"IMF-Supported Programs in Indonesia, Korea and Thailand," IMF Occasional Paper No. 178, June 30, 1999. Fiscal tightening, it states, was intended to restore investor confidence in being repaid, hence reducing pressure on the capital account, and to avoid crowding out the private sector as credit availability declined. In the event, "the thrust of fiscal policy . . . turned out to be substantially different . . . because . . . the original assumptions for economic growth, capital flows, and exchange rates . . . were proved drastically wrong" (page 62). Monetary tightening in Thailand and Korea supported the priority objective of stabilizing the exchange rate, but in Indonesia massive liquidity injections to counter a run on banks led to an explosion in base money and continued currency depreciation (page 38).

August 1998, the international financial system came close to a meltdown. It was avoided only by the timely intervention of the U.S. Federal Reserve.

Where the IMF did have a choice was in pressing emerging economies to open their capital markets. In retrospect it is clear that the international community under the leadership of the U.S. Treasury went too far in that direction. The IMF was even proposing to include the opening of capital markets among its core objectives at the time the Asian crisis erupted. Not much has been heard of that proposal since that time.

THE CURRENT SITUATION

The crisis of 1997–1999 revealed a fundamental flaw in the architecture of the international financial system. The countries at the center of the system are in a position to apply countercyclical policies. For instance, in the current downturn, the United States has aggressively reduced interest rates and cut taxes. But the conditions imposed by the IMF are pro-cyclical: They push countries into recessions by forcing them to raise interest rates and cut budgetary expenditures—exactly the opposite of what the United States is doing in similar circumstances.

In the past, countries with IMF programs were able to recover because financial markets had confidence in the IMF and were willing to follow its lead. For example, Korea was heavily indebted in 1980 and was caught up in the international lending crisis, but it managed to grow itself out of the problem beautifully. Since the 1997–1999 crisis, however, the emperor has no clothes: IMF programs fail to impress the markets. The afflicted countries seem to be caught in a downward cycle.

This problem is not new. It is a feature of the gold standard, and it was at the heart of the Great Depression of the 1930s. The founders of the Bretton Woods institutions, especially Keynes, intended that deficit and surplus countries should be treated symmetrically, both equally obligated to adjust to restore balance. In practice, the IMF's leverage over surplus countries is almost nonexistent, and the burden of adjusting international payments imbalances has fallen almost exclusively on the borrowing countries.

Market fundamentalists see nothing wrong with this because they believe in market discipline. They are reluctant to accept that the system may be fundamentally flawed when it is working so well for those who are in charge. They attribute the crisis of 1997–1999 to struc-

Rich (countries) get richer, and Poor (countries) get poorer

yes

tural faults in the affected countries. Insofar as they acknowledge any systemic defect, they attribute it to the moral hazard introduced by the IMF bailouts.

Undoubtedly there have been structural defects in individual countries, and it is also true that the IMF created a moral hazard, although the case is often overstated. But how will the system work without a moral hazard? The IMF rescue packages have served as a counterweight to the inherent disadvantages of the periphery and allowed the emerging economies to attract capital from abroad. The system does need to be changed, but it is not enough to eliminate the moral hazard. Something else must be put in its place to counterbalance the inherent disadvantages of the periphery and create a more even playing field. That is why I am arguing for credit guarantees and other credit enhancements, as I have been arguing from early on in the crisis.*

The fact is that the moral hazard has already been cured. In the 1997–1999 crisis, the IMF did not succeed in bailing out the banks in Indonesia and Russia, and investors

---

*George Soros, "Avoiding a Breakdown: Asia's Crisis Demands a Rethink of International Regulation," *Financial Times* (London), December 31, 1997, page 12. George Soros, "To Avert the Next Crisis," *Financial Times* (London), January 4, 1999, page 18.

suffered serious losses. Moreover, in the course of the crisis the IMF has shifted its posture by 180 degrees: Instead of bailing out, it now insists on "bailing in" the private sector. The shift occurred gradually: By the time the Russian crisis came to a climax in August 1998, moral hazard had become a politically sensitive issue and constrained the financial authorities in their efforts to avoid the default. Thereafter, the IMF insisted on private sector participation in the rescue package for Brazil. This delayed the process and aggravated the crisis because commercial banks reduced their exposure in anticipation of having to maintain their credit lines. Subsequently, the IMF tried to find a country where it could demonstrate its new policy of private sector burden sharing. It tried in Ukraine and Romania and finally succeeded in Ecuador. The principle is now established and is reflected in the market prices of emerging market debt instruments.

What used to be a theoretical argument appears to be turning into reality. Emerging market economies are suffering from capital outflows *and* higher borrowing costs. Chart 4.1 shows the financial flows to emerging markets. It can be seen that the flow of credit has dropped sharply since 1996. What is less clearly visible, because it is obscured by the innocuous term "resident lending," is that capital flight has offset most of the inflow. Taking resident lending, portfolio investment, and private credit flows together, there has actually been a net outflow from emerging markets since 1997, going from positive $81.7 billion in 1996 to a negative $106 billion in 2000, offset by slightly larger inflows of foreign direct investment and by official financing. Chart 4.2 shows the J. P. Morgan

Chart 4.1: Emerging Market Economies' External Financing (in Billions of Dollars)

	1990	1991	1992	1993	1994
Current Account Balance	-15.5	-20.4	-50.1	-78.2	-70.6
I. Private Inflows					
a. Portfolio investment, net[1]		5.9	13.8	45.4	29.4
b. Private credit, net[2]	22.8	42.6	77.0	96.5	73.4
Subtotal (a + b)	22.8	48.5	90.8	141.9	102.8
II. Resident lending/other[3]	-36.8	-41.5	-59.9	-66.1	-81.0
Subtotal (I + II)	-14.0	7.0	30.9	75.8	21.8
III. Direct investment, net		23.4	31.9	44.8	67.2
IV. Official flows, net	40.4	35.8	35.9	23.4	26.2
Total net external financing (I + II + III + IV)	26.4	66.2	98.7	144.0	115.2

f = forecast
1. Net of outward portfolio investment
2. Net of debt amoritization
3. Net lending, monetary gold, errors and omissions

emerging market bond index (EMBI) from 1991 to 2001. It can be seen that the risk premium has settled at levels significantly higher than those that prevailed prior to the crisis of 1997–1999. The only question is whether the change is temporary or permanent. Market fundamentalists regard it as transitory; I maintain that it is structural.

1995	1996	1997	1998	1999	2000	2001f	2002f
-85,1	-96.1	-76.8	-8.2	23.1	39.2	12.4	
24.4	35.7	25.7	13.6	15.5	16.3	3.8	9.0
123.1	198.7	121.0	8.9	-21.8	20.3	-22.1	10.3
147.5	234.4	146.7	22.5	-6.3	36.6	-18.3	19.3
-90.4	-152.7	-179.9	-146.1	-120.2	-142.6	-99.1	-95.8
57.1	81.7	-33.2	-123.6	-126.5	-106.0	-117.4	-76.5
81.3	93.3	116.1	120.7	147.6	130.2	124.4	108.0
40.9	4.7	36.7	52.4	10.5	-1.3	29.6	20.2
179.3	179.7	119.6	49.5	31.6	22.9	36.6	51.7

Source: Institute of International Finance, Washington, D.C., September 20, 2001.

Chart 4.2: EMBI January 1991–December 2001 Global Sovereign Spread

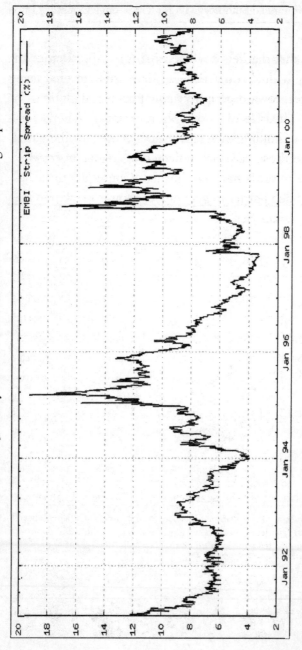

The EMBI Global tracks total return for U.S. dollars-denominated debt instruments issued by emerging market sovereign and quasi-sovereign entities: Brady bonds, loans, Eurobonds, and local market instruments. Countries covered are Algeria, Argentina, Brazil, Bulgaria, Chile, China, Colombia, Cote d'Ivoire, Croatia, Ecuador, Greece, Hungary, Lebanon, Malaysia, Mexico, Morocco, Nigeria, Panama, Peru, the Philippines, Poland, Russia, South Africa, South Korea, Thailand, Turkey, and Venezuela. Source: J. P. Morgan EMBI Index, December 2001.

It is true that markets have become more discriminating among individual countries, but the attitude of the financial markets toward periphery countries is predominantly negative. The risks of lending to or investing in periphery countries or holding their currencies have greatly increased and, since those risks are reflected in higher borrowing costs, the rewards have diminished. Consequently it has become much harder to generate economic growth in the periphery countries, and the lack of progress generates political risks. In another manifestation of the uneven playing field, even the best emerging market companies may have to pay large interest premiums to raise capital, damaging their ability to compete in the global market and making them easy takeover targets for industrial country-based firms.* This holds true for countries as far apart as South Africa, Bulgaria, and Brazil. The high cost or unavailability of capital is the new contagion. It manifests itself not only in the lack of foreign investment but also in the flight of domestic capital. After the crisis of 1997–1999, the world's savings flowed to the United States in search of better investment opportunities; after the bursting of the technology bubble, the inflow continued, motivated by the search for a safe haven. Unlike the

*As the Asian experience shows, when governments try to offset this disadvantage through directed lending or other direct or indirect subsidies to domestic companies, they may sow the seeds of future instability.

periphery, the United States has had no trouble financing its current account deficit, which in 2000 reached 4.4 percent of GDP.* *much bigger now*

What is missing now is a set of incentives to encourage the flow of capital to emerging markets. It is a common occurrence in history that correcting one defect creates another. After World War I, the French built the Maginot Line to put themselves in a better position for trench warfare, and in World War II they were overrun by tanks. Similarly, the shift in IMF policy from bailing out to bailing in was aimed at winning yesterday's war: avoiding a credit crisis by preventing a recurrence of an unsound lending boom. It has succeeded in its objective but has also sown the seeds of the next crisis: an inadequate flow of capital to the emerging markets.

No Miracle Solutions

It is easier to identify the problems than to cure them. I have explained earlier why financial markets are inher-

---

*In 2000, 64 percent of global net capital exports flowed to the United States, compared to an average 35 percent in 1992–1997, according to the IMF's report, *International Capital Markets: Developments, Prospects and Key Policy Issues* (Washington, DC: International Monetary Fund, 2001).

not predictable (but what if there were one international currency + credit?)

ently unstable. There is no magic formula that can change this condition. The financial system offers some excellent examples of problems that have no solutions. It is important to understand them to devise some practical proposals that would minimize their adverse consequences.

The first insoluble problem is the currency regime. Whatever regime prevails is bound to be defective, and the passage of time will reveal the flaw. Fixed exchange rates are too rigid; floating exchange rates are prone to develop self-reinforcing trends that eventually carry them into far-from-equilibrium territory. The major currencies clearly show such patterns. Trends often persist for several years before they are reversed, causing wide and disruptive fluctuations.*

Currency pegs, that is, tying the value of a currency to the dollar, the euro, or a basket of currencies, are also unsustainable. The breakdown of currency pegs in Southeast Asia was the immediate cause of the crisis in 1997. After the crisis, a theory was put forward that the solution is to be found at either of the two extremes or "corners": either a currency board or a free float. Currency boards are more

---

*It has been argued that currency fluctuations are no wider than the price swings in some basic commodities. But that does not change the argument; both are disruptive.

formal and more rigid than currency pegs. Under a currency board the monetary authority is by law prohibited from issuing national currency unless an equivalent amount of hard currency has been deposited with it.

Events have already proven the corner solution theory false. The currency board arrangement placed Argentina in an untenable position, and floating exchange rates have led to the seemingly endless appreciation of the dollar. The only lasting solution would be a single currency, but the world is not ready for it. Even the EU has difficulties managing its single currency, the euro.

The second insoluble problem is the absence of a global central bank. The IMF cannot act as lender of last resort because it does not exercise control over domestic banking systems. Acting in that capacity would mean signing a blank check. The absence of a lender of last resort forces the periphery countries to follow pro-cyclical, anti-Keynesian monetary policies.

De facto, it is the Federal Reserve System and the U.S. Treasury that are in charge of the world's macroeconomic policy, although the other G7 countries also have a voice.*

*IMF staff estimate that a one percentage point increase in U.S. interest rates could reduce developing country GNP by half a percent annually relative to

Being in charge gives the United States a tremendous advantage, although this fact is not usually acknowledged. The U.S. authorities pay considerable attention to conditions abroad, but their primary responsibility is for conditions at home, and in the ultimate analysis that is what guides their actions. When financial markets at the center are threatened they intervene vigorously, but they are able to suffer the pain of periphery countries without flinching.

The benefits that come from being in charge of the system can be demonstrated by contrasting the role of Germany in 1992 with that role today. In 1992, the Bundesbank was in charge of the monetary policy of the European Exchange Rate Mechanism (ERM). The reunification of Germany with a currency exchange rate of essentially 1:1 set up inflationary pressures in Germany while the rest of Europe was suffering from high unemployment and recession. The Bundesbank was duty bound by its constitution to raise interest rates, whereas the rest of Europe needed lower rates. The resulting tensions led to the breakdown of the ERM.

---

baseline forecasts. See V. Aurora and M. Cerisola, *How Does U.S. Monetary Policy Influence Economic Conditions in Emerging Markets?* United States, Selected Issues, IMF Staff Country Report No. 00/1.12 (Washington, DC: International Monetary Fund, 2000).

Today Germany has only one voice in the European Central Bank (ECB). It received no economic stimulus from the introduction of the euro, whereas the periphery countries of the Eurozone—Spain, Italy, and Ireland—benefited from a decline in their domestic interest rates close to the level that prevails at the center, namely Germany. As a consequence, these countries are doing better while the German economy is the weakest within the Eurozone. ECB policy is based on economic conditions in the Eurozone as a whole, and Germany is fast becoming the sick man of Europe. This example goes to show that being in charge of the system confers a definite advantage quite irrespective of being wealthy or not. But of course, being wealthy and powerful tends to put you in charge.

this is all based on free-market economics.

SOME PRACTICAL PROPOSALS

It would be unrealistic to advocate a wholesale change in the prevailing structure of the international financial system. The relative power of individual countries may shift over time, but the United States is not going to abdicate its position, nor will other countries be able to rebel against it. Periphery countries may find it painful to belong to the system, but opting out may be even more painful.

I'm sure that was said about Rome. What time frame?

132

It is not unrealistic, however, to advocate some improvements in the prevailing arrangements. Open society is an imperfect society that holds itself open to improvement. The present financial architecture certainly qualifies as imperfect, and it would benefit all members, including the United States, to improve it. Some countries like Argentina and Turkey have been hovering on the brink of disaster, and other periphery countries are suffering from high risk premiums and lack of investment flows. Conditions in the rest of the world have become a matter of grave concern for the financial authorities at the center.

I have already proposed an important improvement in chapter 2: the use of SDRs for providing international assistance. This could serve to reduce the disparity between center and periphery; it could also serve as a countercyclical policy tool that could turn out to be particularly valuable if the world economy slipped into deflation. Here I want to probe deeper and examine what other improvements could be made to the international financial system.

We can identify two major deficiencies or, more exactly, asymmetries in the way the IMF has been operating until recently. One is a disparity between crisis prevention and crisis intervention; the other is a disparity in the treatment of lenders and borrowers.

The general principles that structural reforms in the IMF ought to follow are clear. There ought to be a better balance between crisis prevention and intervention and a better balance between offering incentives to countries that follow sound policies and penalizing those that do not. The two objectives are connected: It is only by offering incentives that the IMF can exert stronger influence on the economic policies of individual countries prior to a country turning to the IMF in a crisis.

These general principles have received widespread recognition, but they have not been properly implemented because market fundamentalism has stood in the way. Instead of devising an appropriate set of sticks and carrots, the monetary authorities have relied on market discipline to a greater extent than appropriate. Their approach could be justified if financial markets in fact tended toward equilibrium, but now that multiple equilibria have become an accepted part of economic theory, that belief is no longer tenable. Market discipline provides the stick but the carrots are missing—although not totally.

The IMF has made some progress in the area of prevention by introducing Contingency Credit Lines (CCLs). The CCL rewards countries following sound policies by giving them access to IMF credit lines before rather than after a crisis has erupted. Unfortunately, the desire for crisis prevention clashed with the emphasis on market discipline, and the latter won out: The original terms were too restrictive and expensive to attract any takers. The conditions were recently modified to make the facility more attractive. Nevertheless, there are still no takers.

The IMF and its major shareholders ought to actively promote the use of CCLs. The Fund has plenty of liquidity; it should be put to more active use. If necessary, the IMF should be provided with additional capital.

In addition to the CCL, other steps could be taken to strengthen the incentives for good policies and to reduce the imbalance between center and periphery. Several alternatives may be considered:

(i)   The IMF could rate countries. The highest grade would make a country automatically eligible for CCLs at little or no cost, and bondholders would be given an assurance that in case of an IMF program their claims would be fully respected. This would provide a powerful enhancement of the country's credit. By contrast, for countries in the lowest grade, the IMF would make it clear in advance that it would not be willing to enter into a program without private sector burden sharing. Caveat emptor: Buyer beware. There could be one or more intermediate grades where the IMF may insist on various degrees of burden sharing.

(ii) The Basel Accord, which sets internationally agreed capital standards for commercial banks, could translate the IMF ratings into variations in capital requirements for commercial bank loans.

(iii) The Federal Reserve, the ECB, the Bank of England (BOE), and the Bank of Japan (BOJ) could accept at their discount windows designated treasury bill issues of selected countries. This privilege could be reserved for specific countries or particularly perilous situations. For instance, after Argentina defaulted, the privilege could have been extended to other Latin American countries that followed sound policies. This would prevent contagion from spreading to countries such as Brazil, Chile, or even Mexico.

(iv) To push the outside of the envelope even further—perhaps too far—the same central banks could also accept at their discount windows longer term bonds of selected countries, imposing discounts that may vary from time to time. This would shrink risk premiums and help periphery countries to lengthen the maturity of their debt. Even more important, it would enable them to pursue countercyclical policies—provided the central banks set the discounts at suitable levels.

(v) Alternatively, the Federal Reserve, the ECB, the BOE, and the BOJ could agree to conduct open market operations using the safest tranches of government paper issued by periphery countries with the highest Fund rating.

These arrangements would help alleviate both asymmetries at the same time. The IMF would be in a better position to prevent crises from developing because it would be one of the requirements for a high rating that there should be a ceiling on a country's short-term obligations. The country concerned would be obliged to collect and publish adequate data on foreign borrowings. This would allow the IMF to monitor the debt profile of individual countries more intensely, and it could downgrade them if macroeconomic conditions deteriorate.* At the same time, there would be a better balance in the

*In 1997, the Korean central bank kept no record of loans of less than 12 months' maturity. The bulk of the loans outstanding fell into that category, aggravating the crisis. There is a new IMF data disclosure standard that includes

don't we trying to save them?

treatment of lenders and borrowers. Countries that follow sound policies would enjoy credit enhancements, while lenders to poorly rated countries would be exposed to greater risks. *How is that can improvement or incentive?*

It is noteworthy that only one of these proposals, namely varying the capital requirements of commercial banks, was seriously considered, and even that discussion has taken a somewhat different direction. The Basel Committee on Banking Supervision has accepted the idea of rating countries, but would let sophisticated financial institutions rely to a large extent on their own internal risk evaluations to determine the amount of capital to be allocated to their sovereign loans. Less sophisticated financial institutions could rely on commercial credit rating agencies instead.*

The proposal to have the IMF rate its members has encountered strenuous opposition. Some argue that the IMF would not dare to downgrade a country because

frequent and detailed public reporting of long- and short-term debt. Korea subscribes, as do more and more IMF members. The annual Article IV report reviews how close a country is to meeting the standard and what the gaps are. However, good data on private sector debt are still hard to come by, even for industrial countries.

*The Basel Committee on Banking Supervision is a consultative body of central banks and bank supervisors of the Group of 10 countries of Europe, Canada, Japan, and the United States.

doing so might precipitate the crisis it was supposed to prevent. But the IMF has an institutional interest in preserving the system, and precipitating a crisis sooner rather than later would reduce its severity. Alternatively, it is argued that the IMF would be prevented from downgrading a country by political pressures. But the IMF would be on solid ground in resisting such pressures because if it made a misjudgment, it would be obligated to put its own resources at risk.

Another objection is that a dividing line between countries that do and do not get a high rating would create too much of a discontinuity. But the monetary authorities would have many means at their disposal to mitigate the discontinuity. They could vary the amounts of treasury bills they are willing to discount, or they could vary the discount rate on the paper. The Basel Accord could impose different capital requirements on bank loans in accordance with IMF rankings.

But the main opposition has come from market fundamentalists who are preoccupied with the issue of moral hazard. Wouldn't a system of IMF guarantees encourage unsound lending? The answer is no. If unsound lending caused a crisis, then the IMF would have to accept the consequences and provide assistance. The IMF would be taking a real risk, not creating a moral hazard. This is another instance where the concept of moral hazard is overused.

The most potent objection is that the IMF lacks the methodology for distinguishing between sound and unsound economic policies. I accept the validity of this objection, especially in light of recent developments. After a flawed performance in the 1997–1999 crisis and now under attack from all sides, the IMF seems to have lost its way. I am not in a position to design the methodology the IMF ought to use in rating individual countries, but I have no doubt that the IMF itself would be able to do so if it were given the responsibility for it. After all, national central banks also lacked the appropriate methodology when they were first entrusted with preventing financial crises and keeping their economies on an even keel, but they developed it and became very successful at their job; the same would most likely happen with the IMF. Indeed, the IMF has already taken an important step toward more objective and vigorous assessments by introducing codes and standards for key components of policy performance and financial soundness, working closely with institutions like the Bank for International Settlements and the Basel Committee on Banking Supervision.

Before the steps advocated here could be introduced,

some important legal issues would have to be resolved. At present, there are no bankruptcy procedures for sovereign debt; as a result, the IMF has no legal powers to impose any burden sharing on the private sector. A debt reorganization scheme mandated by the IMF would probably not be approved by the courts, at least U.S. courts, which govern a large part of international debt issues, unless it was also approved by the bondholders. But the mechanism for gaining approval is missing. Only around one-quarter of international bonds issued by emerging market borrowers contain collective action clauses limiting the ability of dissident bondholders to block a reorganization. Such clauses are not allowed under U.S. law.

Introducing bankruptcy court–type protection from creditors would probably require amending the IMF Articles of Agreement to clarify its standing to effect a standstill.* The investment community has opposed such an amendment up to now. However, bondholders and investment banks would have little cause for complaint if the new

---

*Article VIII.2.b gives the Fund the power to sanction capital and exchange controls that could prohibit and limit the availability of foreign exchange for certain payments overseas, but there are questions about the IMF's legal jurisdiction in this area vis-à-vis national contract law. Courts in different countries have given different interpretations. For a summary of these issues, see "Resolving and Preventing Financial Crises: The Role of the Private Sector," An IMF Issues Brief, March 26, 2001.

standstill rules were accompanied by the credit enhancements outlined above.

The IMF, with support and encouragement from the U.S. Treasury, is now giving serious consideration to the creation of an international bankruptcy mechanism.* But there has been no consideration of the credit enhancements proposed in this book. That is a pity because the two measures would be easier to implement in conjunction with each other than a bankruptcy procedure without sweeteners.

The issue is pressing. Argentina has defaulted. The handwriting has been on the wall for a long time, and financial markets could clearly read the message, especially as it was in their own handwriting. The only question was whether it was going to be an orderly debt reorganization or a disorderly one. The answer depended largely but not entirely on whether the IMF could provide assistance to an orderly reduction of the debt burden against the objections of dissident bondholders. There were of course other conditions that Argentina would have had to meet to qualify for international assistance, but it was the

*Anne Krueger, First Deputy Managing Director of the International Monetary Fund, Address to the National Economists' Club Annual Members' Dinner, American Enterprise Institute, Washington, D.C., November 26, 2001.

absence of clarity on this issue that stood in the way of a meaningful dialogue.

To say that the Argentine default turned out to be disorderly may be an understatement. The full implications of what has happened have not yet sunk in. Argentina's former economy minister, Domingo Cavallo, sacrificed practically everything on the altar of maintaining the currency board and meeting international obligations. The integrity of the domestic pension and banking systems was impaired and there was no refuge for domestic savings. When the break came it was a violent one as people rioted and the government fell. There was no fallback position and the financial system completely seized up. The consequences are disastrous for Argentina and there will also be some adverse repercussions for the international financial system—although these are not yet recognized by the financial markets. The first reaction of the markets was one of relief at the almost complete absence of contagion. The default was so predictable that it had been fully discounted. However, its longer-term consequences are yet to be felt. Foreign direct investments—banks, utilities, and oil companies—have been badly hurt. The extensive violation of contracts will endanger foreign direct investment, which had hitherto been considered the most stable and dependable element in capital flows to emerging markets. The contagion will be slow because direct investments move much more slowly than other financial assets, but it is likely to spread. Spanish banks and utilities that are hurt in Argentina are likely to retrench in other emerging markets, especially if the stock market penalizes them for their overseas exposure; and other direct investors, particularly in the financial sector, are bound to be influenced by their fate. How far the general retrenchment may go will depend to a large extent on the policy response.

Turmoil in Argentina is likely to bring matters to a head. The flaw in current arrangements, namely the increasing shortage of capital and the consequent rise in risk premiums for periphery countries will become more acute. The issue of how a sovereign default can be handled in an orderly manner will have to be resolved. The likely outcome is some kind of international bankruptcy procedure. This will impair the discipline that sustains international lending because, in contrast to corporate borrowers, sovereign states do not provide any tangible security; the only security the lender has is the pain that the borrower will suffer if it defaults. That is why the private sector has been so strenuously opposed to any measure that would reduce the pain, whether it is collective action clauses in sovereign bonds or the IMF "lending into arrears." Collective action clauses allow a majority of bondholders to overrule the objections of a few dissidents in agreeing to a debt reorganization. Lending into arrears is a principle introduced since the emerging market crisis that allows the IMF to lend to countries that are in arrears to their bondholders. Both these initiatives are part of the new approach to moral hazard, insisting on bailing-in the private sector instead of bailing it out. Argentina will have cured the moral hazard for good, but it will have also demonstrated the devastation that can be wrought by a disorderly default.

Whether an international bankruptcy procedure is introduced or not, the lack of capital availability in emerging markets will become impossible to ignore, and the credit enhancements I have proposed will have to be considered. Thus the Argentine crisis may well turn out to be the catalyst that will bring the new financial architecture that I am advocating here into existence. It will differ from the present state of affairs by offering more carrots to periphery countries pursuing sound policies.

As mentioned previously, deciding what constitutes sound policy presents the toughest challenge. The Argentine crisis provides an excellent example. On the whole, Argentina followed macroeconomic policies that were in accordance with IMF orthodoxy. Its troubles stemmed from a currency board system that was approved by the IMF at the time of its creation but subsequently led to a currency misalignment. It made sense to insist on a currency realignment, but the Argentine government and much of its public opinion were firmly wedded to the currency board arrangement: They were determined not to return to a floating exchange rate that pushed Argentina into decades of currency depreciation. Moreover, monetary stability was the only achievement they had to show for years of painful recession. This placed the IMF and the U.S. Treasury in a predicament: whether to endorse a policy that they considered unsound or to allow Argentina to go into default. At first, they opted for the first alternative, but eventually they switched to the second. The sequence had the quality of a Greek tragedy.

This goes to show that there are no perfect solutions to the problems of the international financial system. Whatever solutions we devise, new problems are bound to arise. I am afraid that the proposals I have put forward here will also prove to be inadequate when they are implemented. Indeed, they seem to be puny when compared with the magnitude of the problems that they are supposed to resolve.

I do not see any point in proposing more radical solutions

when the authorities are not ready to consider even the moderate ones outlined here. First they must realize that financial markets do not tend toward equilibrium; financial markets need a visible hand to guide them and keep them from going off the rails. Today the visible hand is that of the United States, supported by the Washington consensus. This has created a very uneven playing field. To ask for an even playing field is utopian; there has never been one. But it is not too much to ask to make the playing field less uneven; that would serve the interests of all parties.

Once this line of argument becomes the official line of the G7 governments, the meager reforms I have proposed here could go a long way in making the international financial system more stable and more equitable. For instance, as suggested, accepting the paper of sound periphery countries at the discount windows of the major central banks could significantly reduce their cost of borrowing. That will not be the end of the road. We shall have to continue to improve our institutional arrangements indefinitely because perfection is beyond our reach.

Toward a
Global Open Society

September 11 was a traumatic experience. The idea that terrorists were willing to kill a large number of innocent civilians and kill themselves in the process shocked all of us. The attack was incredibly audacious, and its effects surpassed even the perpetrators' expectations. Television brought the event into people's homes, and people were terrorized. The illusion that the United States is invulnerable was shattered.

A traumatic event of this kind affects people on two levels: the instinctual and the rational. If the trauma is strong enough the two levels may become temporarily disconnected. With the passage of time reason regains the upper hand, but the memory remains. We are still wrestling to come to terms with it. Our view of the world has been shaken, and we are actively engaged in rearranging it.

People in the United States have been forced to realize that others may regard them very differently from the way they see themselves. They have become aware that what happens abroad can affect them directly. This creates an unusual opportunity to reassess the role that the United States plays in the world. In the previous chapters, I dealt with the IFTIs; here I shall focus on the role of the United States more directly.

As the analysis in this book has shown, the United States occupies a dominant position in the global economy. Insofar as anybody is in charge of economic policy it is the United States. The United States cannot do anything it wants, but practically nothing can happen without its consent.

The American response to September 11 has demonstrated that the United States is also the dominant military power in the world. Its military superiority is greater than ever. It can do in a few weeks what the Soviet Union could not do in years: impose its will on Afghanistan. And it can do it from halfway around the world. The bombs have gotten much smarter since Desert Storm. With its military and economic power combined, the United States is the unquestioned hegemon in the world today.

Hegemony carries with it tremendous responsibility.

Other countries have to respond to U.S. policy, but the United States is in a position to choose the policy to which others have to respond. Our control over our destiny is of course limited. We act on the basis of imperfect understanding, and our actions have unintended consequences. Outcomes rarely correspond to expectations. But subject to that limitation we have a greater degree of discretion in deciding what shape the world should take than anybody else. It is fortunate that the people have started to think about foreign policy; as a result, the United States may live up to its responsibilities as it has often done in the past—I am thinking of the Marshall Plan, for instance.

The position of the United States was not very different before September 11 than afterwards—although the Afghan campaign was an impressive demonstration of our military might. But Americans were only vaguely aware of their dominant position. They thought they were competing on a level playing field and all their efforts went into competition. Only a decade ago there were many voices warning that the United States was losing out to Japan. So it was a great comfort and a source of pride that the United States came out ahead.

The underlying principle of globalization is competition. As globalization took hold, competition got tougher.

There was no time to think beyond one's own economic position, and there was no point in questioning a system that was obviously working to our benefit. The terrorist attack on September 11 changed all that. People feel a need to understand how it could have happened; and when they start to think about the world in which they live, they must become aware of the dominant position that the United States occupies.

Once we recognize our hegemonic position and the discretion it gives us to shape the world in which we live, the question presents itself: How should we use that discretion?

I shall sketch out two alternative visions of the U.S. role in the world. They are not really alternatives; reality is bound to be some kind of a compromise between the two. By presenting them as alternatives I hope to bring into sharper focus the choices that confront us.

The two visions are not really new. They have exerted an influence on American policy throughout its history. I shall call them *geopolitical realism* and *open society idealism*. Henry Kissinger points out that the United States has been almost unique among nations in allowing a strong streak of idealism to permeate its foreign policy. That has to do with its origin: The United States was founded with the Declaration of Independence, which is an eloquent expression of the universal principles of what I call the open society.*

Geopolitical realism is based on the interests of the state; open society idealism stresses the interests of humanity. Ever since the Enlightenment, there has always been a tension between universal principles and the sovereignty of the state. As the United States grew stronger the tension became more pronounced. Theodore Roosevelt can be taken as the protagonist of American hegemony and Woodrow Wilson stands for an idealistic approach to international affairs. He does not qualify, however, as a paragon of open society idealism because of his dismal civil rights record at home. Jimmy Carter is a purer example. When geopolitical realism and open society idealism clash, the former usually wins out.

The Cold War can be interpreted as a conflict between two superpowers or as a conflict between two ideas about how society ought to be organized: open society and

*The expression "open society" was not known at the time of the Declaration of Independence. The term was first used by Henri Bergson in 1932 in *Two Sources of Religion and Morality*. One source is tribal and supports a closed society; the other is universal and gives rise to an open society.

closed society. Actually, it was both. The Cold War was one of those periods in American history when the two visions blended together more or less harmoniously. (World War II was another after the United States joined it.) There were of course sharp differences during the Cold War on which vision should take precedence; at the time of the Vietnam War they clashed quite explicitly. But if one takes the near half century of the Cold War as a whole, the United States successfully combined the two roles of being one of the two superpowers and the leader of the free world. Other democratic countries voluntarily submitted to U.S. leadership in face of a common danger. Most important, the United States emerged victorious.

After the collapse of communism and the disintegration first of the Soviet empire and then the Soviet Union itself, the choice between the two visions presented itself more starkly. Strangely enough, American public opinion was hardly aware of it. Under the influence of market fundamentalism, the idea of reaching out to the formerly communist countries the way the United States reached out to Europe after the end of World War II with the Marshall Plan did not even come into consideration. (I felt quite alone when I threw all my resources into helping the formerly communist countries to make the transition to open societies.) As a result, a historic opportunity was lost, but the American public remains unaware of it to this day. The United States chose the path of geopolitical realism almost unthinkingly.

After September 11, the American public has become more aware than before that what happens in the rest of the world can affect them directly and there are important foreign policy choices to be made. This awareness may not last long, and I am determined not to let the moment pass.

It has to be bluntly stated that the path chosen by the United States proved to be highly successful. We enjoy a dominant position both from an economic and a military point of view. The natural tendency, the line of least resistance, leads to a continuation of market fundamentalism and geopolitical realism. It has worked: We have established undisputed leadership and we ought to do whatever it takes to preserve it. We are on top and we must stay there. Competition is the guiding principle in both economic and military matters, and the goal is to come out ahead.

This goal is best served in the economic sphere by removing all obstacles from the pursuit of profit. Having a large market and a sound legal system that protects property rights, we can attract capital and entrepreneurship by offering a hospitable environment for business. The EU offers an even larger market and an equally sound legal system, but the environment is far less hospitable to business. Labor markets are rigid, with greater restrictions on employing and dismissing people, and there are all kinds of other regulations. Capital is in fact drawn to the United States from Europe and from all over the world. The United States has a current account deficit of more than 4 percent of the GDP, yet the dollar has been going from strength to strength.

Being in possession of the main trading currency and in charge of its own economic policy, it is very much in U.S. interests to have open markets, particularly financial markets. That is in fact the policy that the United States has pursued, sometimes with disastrous effects for countries whose financial systems could not operate efficiently in a competitive environment. Japan, for instance, had built up a very efficient industrial system, but its financial system was geared not to obey market signals but to take instructions from the Ministry of Finance. When financial markets opened up, the financial system frittered away the wealth that the industrial system generated. Japan is mired in a financial crisis from which it seems incapable of extricating itself.

Having open markets can sometimes be detrimental to particular industries, but the United States is powerful enough to impose trade restrictions when the pain—and the political pressure—become too heavy. This has been facilitated by the unequal influence of developed and developing countries within the structure of the WTO. It can be seen that globalization has worked for the United States like a charm, and it has been pursued by both political parties although their policies may have differed in some details.

The United States has also continued to maintain a strong military posture since the end of the Cold War. The size of the armed forces was reduced, but there was no let up in technological innovation. The gap between the military capabilities of the United States and the rest of the world has become wider than ever. This is reflected in budgets: The United States accounts for 37 percent of the world's total military spending.*

In military matters there is a significant difference between the Bush and Clinton administrations. President Bush is determined to exploit the technological advantage the United States currently enjoys and to push ahead without letting international agreements stand in the way. NATO has lost much of its usefulness since the end of the Cold War; it has become one of those multilateral institutions

*This information comes from the Stockholm International Peace Research Institute.

that the United States holds in low esteem. The National Missile Defense (NMD), by contrast, holds out the promise of reestablishing the unilateral control that the United States enjoyed during the Cold War but this time without an adversary capable of inflicting total destruction. The Bush administration came into office with the determination to pursue NMD against all opposition, and it has not been diverted from this course by September 11. The Clinton administration was much more ambivalent on this issue; it delayed taking a decision until after the elections.

It has to be admitted that the Bush administration's policy is internally much more consistent than that of the Clinton administration. It is unabashedly unilateralist and hegemonic, whereas President Clinton mixed a hard-headed pursuit of economic competitiveness with a rather sentimental attachment to peacemaking in international affairs. A strong defense posture combines well with a reliance on market discipline in the economic sphere to ensure overall American hegemony.

Politically, the terrorist attack provided the Bush administration with the enemy it needed to justify its strong defense posture. Prior to September 11, the administration was looking high and low for an enemy against whom NMD could be regarded as a defense. It deemed North

Korea suitable for that role at least for the near term, and President Bush pressed South Korean President Kim Dae Jung to stop trying to bring North Korea in from the cold. For the longer term the administration was positioning China as a potential strategic rival, but even Russia was not left out of consideration. The terrorist attack provided an instant solution. President Bush did not hesitate to declare war on terrorism, and the nation lined up behind the president. It is difficult to see how NMD can protect against terrorist attacks, but with the degree of support he is currently enjoying, the president has no difficulty in renouncing the Anti-Ballistic Missile Treaty and pushing ahead with NMD.

Terrorism is the ideal enemy because it is invisible and therefore does not disappear. The need for other enemies has dissipated, and relations with China and Russia have undergone a remarkable transformation. This is one of several positive by-products of one of the most devastating tragedies in American history. Having an enemy that poses a genuine and widely recognized threat can be very effective in holding the nation together. That is particularly useful when the prevailing ideology is based on the unabashed pursuit of self-interest.

But the situation is not without its dangers. In a state of

war the president is largely immune from criticism. Yet a critical process is the foundation of an open society. At present, the critical process is practically in abeyance. The Democratic opposition is loathe to criticize the president, and the attorney general has gone so far as to declare any opposition to the antiterrorist measures an unpatriotic act that gives aid and comfort to the enemy.* Open society is under duress in the United States. Somewhat less obviously, we may be once again missing a historic opportunity to move toward a global open society.

It is difficult to engage in a critical examination of administration policies at a time of genuine emergency when the government is doing many things that need to be done. Rather than trying to find faults, I shall try to explain the historic opportunity we are missing.

We are the dominant economic and military power in the world today. We have a large degree of discretion in setting the terms of the discussion about globalization and

---

*"To those who pit Americans against immigrants, citizens against non-citizens, those who scare peace-loving people with phantoms of lost liberty, my message is this: Your tactics only aid terrorists for they erode our national unity and diminish our resolve. They give ammunition to America's enemies and pause to America's friends. They encourage people of good will to remain silent in the face of evil." Testimony of Attorney General John Ashcroft before the United States Senate Judiciary Committee, December 6, 2001.

the future of the world in general. We are missing a historic opportunity when we focus all our efforts on perpetuating our dominant position. The United States ought to pay a lot more attention to the functioning of the global capitalist system and the fate of humanity as a whole. It needs to do so both for its own sake and for the welfare and survival of humanity. It is not something that the United States can or should do on its own. A cooperative effort is needed but it cannot be done without U.S. leadership.

Our hegemony is quite secure. On the military side it would take decades before another state could challenge us. The country most likely to want to do so is China, which seeks to assert its sovereignty over Taiwan. But China is lagging far behind Russia in military technology, particularly in the air. The two powers that would be closest to being able to challenge our military superiority are the EU and Russia. But the EU is not yet a military power at all, and the various states that compose it are allied closely with the United States in NATO. Russia is primarily interested in economic development. It seeks to regain great power status partly for the sake of its own identity and partly because it may be a good investment, but it will not repeat the Soviet experiment of sacrificing economic prosperity and advancement for the sake of superpower status. At first the Bush administration treated Russia coldly; after September 11 the relationship underwent a notable warming. The basis of the new relationship is almost entirely geopolitical. Both sides know how to play the game, but it is the United States that sets the terms. We may not be aware of it, but the United States has a great influence over what kind of game Russia will be playing in the future.

In the economic sphere, U.S. dominance is somewhat less secure, but the threats come more from the system itself than from the position of the United States within the system. The fact that there is a synchronous global recession has put the system under great stress, and whatever can go wrong is liable to do so. But the U.S. economy is much stronger than that of the rest of the world and U.S. leadership is difficult to challenge.*

Although no state can challenge American supremacy, we are at risk if we fail to live up to the responsibilities that our leadership position imposes. That is the real significance of September 11: It has brought home the fact that

*For example, at the height of the Asian financial crisis, Eisuke Sakakibara, who was then in charge of the Japanese Ministry of Finance, proposed creating an Asian Monetary Fund with significant resources. Under pressure from the United States, the plan was soon dropped.

we are at risk. It is fashionable to speak of asymmetric threats. What makes them asymmetric is that they do not fit neatly into the equations of geopolitical realism.

The risks that confront us cannot be understood in terms of the disciplines we have relied on to establish our supremacy: market discipline and geopolitical realism. Both disciplines relate to power. But the responsibilities I am talking about are moral responsibilities. That is the missing ingredient in U.S. policy. It is of course not entirely missing; it is only shunted to the sidelines by the prevailing doctrines of market fundamentalism and geopolitical realism.

We have come to distrust invocations of moral principles because those principles are easily perverted. It is difficult to distinguish between right and wrong and even more difficult to reach consensus on what is right. It is much easier to find a moral justification for amoral or immoral behavior. Morality breeds hypocrisy and lends itself to abuse. Many heinous acts have been committed in its name. September 11 is one of the worst examples.

We have been so put off by the perversion of morality that we are trying to do without morality. The distinguishing feature of both market fundamentalism and geopolitical realism is that they are *amoral*—morality does not enter into the calculations. That is one of the reasons why they have been so successful. We have been seduced by their success into thinking that we can do without moral considerations. We have come to worship success. We admire businessmen who make a fortune and politicians who get themselves elected irrespective of how they have done it.

That is where we have gone wrong. No society can exist without morality. Even our amoral pursuits need a moral justification. Market fundamentalists claim that the un-trammeled pursuit of self-interest serves the common interest; and the exercise of our geopolitical power appeals to our patriotism. The fact remains that these are amoral pursuits. If that is all we have to offer, our view of the world is liable to be rejected by more traditional societies where morality still plays a central role. That is the case in traditional Islamic societies where church and state have not even been separated. In the end, we may not find it satisfactory ourselves.

When I speak of morality I do not mean it in the tradi-tional sense of observing religious precepts or standards of propriety. Those are private matters in societies where church and state are separated. I mean accepting the responsibilities that go with belonging to a global com-munity. Those responsibilities are not well defined at present. Our international arrangements are based on the sovereignty of states, and states are guided by their own interests that do not necessarily coincide with the interests of the people who live in those states and are even less likely to coincide with the interests of humanity as a whole. Those latter interests need to be better protected than they are at present.

The lesson we have to learn from September 11 is that morality has to play a larger role in international affairs. The asymmetric threats that confront us arise out of the asymmetry that we have identified in globalization: We have global markets but we do not have a global society. And we cannot build a global society without taking into account moral considerations.

In saying this I am of course not excusing terrorism in any shape or form. What I am asserting is that the moral base of globalization and American domination is deficient. Markets are amoral, the untrammeled pursuit of self-interest does not necessarily serve the common interest, and military might is not necessarily right. This may be an unpopular thing to say, especially after innocent people have been killed in the name of a perverted religious belief, but it is nevertheless true. I was saying it before September 11.

The United States bears a special responsibility for the world because of its dominant position. Without its cooperation no international arrangements are possible. Yet the United States is the major obstacle to international cooperation today. It is resolutely opposed to any international arrangement that would infringe on its sovereignty. The list is long, including the International Criminal Court, the Landmines Treaty, the Kyoto Protocol, many of the ILO conventions, and many more arcane conventions like the Law of the Sea Convention and the Convention on Biological Diversity. The United States is one of only nine nations that have not ratified the latter convention. The only area where the United States is willing to subordinate its sovereignty to international institutions is in the facilitation of international commerce. Prior to September 11 the Bush administration was not even willing to accept OECD standards for monitoring financial transactions. After September 11, it is still not willing to compromise its sovereignty in waging war on terrorists. Under UN rules, it is not obliged to do so because it can claim to be acting in self-defense.

It is here that the pursuit of hegemony comes into direct conflict with the vision of a global open society. The hegemonic view is willing to tolerate infringements of the sovereignty of other states but insists on protecting U.S. sovereignty in all its aspects. It wants the United States to be the unmoved mover. The vision of a global open society requires the United States to abide by the same rules that apply to others. Moreover, it requires the United States to exercise leadership in strengthening our international institutions, rules, laws, and standards. Since the sovereignty of states stands in the way of enforcing most rules, laws, and standards, it must be willing to offer inducements and incentives for voluntary compliance. Of course the United States cannot be expected to do that on its own, but it must take the initiative to secure the cooperation of other countries.

It hardly needs mentioning that this vision is radically opposed to current U.S. policy. This is not a matter of party politics. The Bush administration is more consistent in its hegemonic views than the Clinton administration was, but the policy is bipartisan—and those who are more sympathetic to the vision of a global open society are also to be found in both parties.

The hegemonic view is considered hard-headed and realistic while the vision of a global open society is liable to be dismissed as utopian. I beg to differ. I admit that the hegemonic view is realistic in the sense that it represents the here and now, but as a goal to pursue it is more unrealistic and counterproductive than a global open society.

No hegemony can be maintained if the dominant member does not pay adequate attention to the interests of the other members, because the other members will combine to break the hegemony. That is the basis of the balance of powers theory espoused by that champion of geopolitical realism, Henry Kissinger. What we have now is much more favorable to the United States than a balance of powers; we enjoy supremacy. By failing to live up to its responsibilities, we are liable to degrade ourselves to a more lowly position within a balance of powers system—not a very alluring prospect. Of course, it is not likely to happen soon because our hegemony is so secure. We can afford to act irresponsibly because it will take decades before other states will be able to form a countervailing force.

That is where the so-called asymmetric threats come into play. If other states are not strong enough to create a balance, people may rebel against the system. Geopolitical realism is ill-suited to deal with asymmetric threats because it is based on the relationship among states, not what happens within states.

The system may be strong enough to repress those asymmetric threats, but repressing them rather than removing the root causes is likely to change the character of the sys-

tem: It would be based on repression rather than cooperation. That would be the result of carrying the hegemonic
view to its logical conclusion. History shows that no
repressive regime can endure forever—although some
have lasted a very long time. Empires that had staying
power found ways to satisfy the needs and aspirations of
the people who belonged to them—the Roman, British,
and Ottoman empires come to mind; those that relied on
repression did not last long—Nazi Germany and the
Soviet Union can be used as examples. That is why I consider the hegemonic view counterproductive. Of course,
the United States could never become like Nazi Germany
or the Soviet Union because our system of government
would not permit it; I am only pointing out the dangers
inherent in the hegemonic view.

By the same token, the vision of a global open society is
very far from utopian. Open society is based on the recognition that we act on the basis of imperfect understanding.
Perfection is beyond our reach; we must content ourselves
with an imperfect society that holds itself open to improvement. The acceptance of imperfection coupled with a
constant search for improvement and a willingness to submit to critical examination are the guiding principles of an
open society. These principles imply that what is real may
not be reasonable—that is to say, the regimes that prevail

are liable to be flawed and therefore in need of reform, and what is reasonable may not be attainable—that is to say, improvements must be based on what exists and what is possible, not on the dictates of some abstract rationality.

The principles of open society find expression in a democratic form of government and a market economy. But in trying to apply these principles on a global scale we run into a seemingly insuperable difficulty: the sovereignty of states.

Sovereignty is an anachronistic concept. It has its origin in the Treaty of Westphalia (1648) concluded after 30 years of religious warfare. It was decided that the sovereign could determine the religion of his subjects: *cuius regio eius religio*. When the people rose up against their rulers in the French Revolution the power they captured was the power of the sovereign. That is how the modern nation-state was born, in which sovereignty belongs to the people. There has been a tension between the nation-state and the universal principles of liberty, equality, and fraternity ever since.

It may be anachronistic, but the concept of sovereignty remains the foundation of international relations. It has to be accepted as the starting point in creating a global open society. States may cede part of their sovereignty by international treaty. The member states of the EU have gone quite far in surrendering their sovereignty. The future of the EU will show how far it is possible to go along that avenue.

One way to foster open societies without running afoul of the sovereignty of states is to offer countries positive incentives for voluntary compliance with international rules and standards. That is the idea that permeates the practical proposals I have put forward in this book. After September 11, it seems appropriate to push this idea a step further.

I have proposed in my previous book, *Open Society*, forming a coalition of the willing with the dual objective of promoting open societies in individual countries and laying the groundwork of a global open society. After September 11 the principle that it is in the common interest of open societies to foster the development of democracy, market economy, and the rule of law in other countries should be generally accepted. There is also a need to establish certain standards of behavior ranging from not harboring terrorists to not manufacturing weapons of mass destruction. None of this will work, of course, without appropriate inspection and enforcement mechanisms.

The need is pressing. The introduction of biological weapons is an irreversible development, similar to the dropping of the first nuclear bomb.

The United States must take the lead. It can choose to act unilaterally or multilaterally. It would be utopian to think that the United States could accomplish these goals unilaterally, yet this is seriously contemplated. It is generally agreed that Saddam Hussein has engaged in the manufacture of biological weapons, and his regime presents a real danger to the world. The question is, What can be done about it? Some elements in the Bush administration argue for the United States attacking Iraq. But even if a military campaign against Iraq were as successful as the campaign against Afghanistan, the problem would not go away. Other countries could engage in the manufacture of biological weapons. Significantly, no elements in the Bush administration are arguing publicly for a multilateral approach. Yet it is the only one that has a chance of success.

The Bush administration refused to complete negotiations to update the 1972 Biological and Toxic Weapons Convention because it considered the inspection features too intrusive and other aspects ineffective; it must now propose a stronger one. The new multilateral treaty should impose on all countries, whether they signed the treaty or not, rigorous inspection requirements. The signatories of the treaty should agree to take whatever measures are necessary against countries that refuse. Saddam Hussein would either have to submit or take the consequences.

It would be desirable to conclude such a treaty under the aegis of the United Nations, but if that proved impossible it should still be possible to form a coalition of the willing that would be strong enough to enforce its will. Naturally the United States and the other signatories would have to abide by the same rules they seek to impose on others.

The question of what to do about nuclear weapons also needs to be addressed with renewed intensity. The present arrangements are unstable. There is a nuclear nonproliferation treaty, but it is not a long-term solution because it is trying to preserve a situation of inequality. It has created a club of nuclear haves who seek to keep the nuclear have-nots out of the club. Originally, the members promised to impose constraints on themselves, but they failed to deliver on their promise. At the same time, they failed to put in effect an enforcement mechanism. This has created an incentive for have-nots to join the club, and if they have the will to develop nuclear weapons it is only a matter of time before the existing members will acquiesce. India and Pakistan have proved the point. The larger the membership the easier it will be to break into the club.

By contrast, the situation was much more stable during the Cold War. Two sides were facing each other, and each had the capacity to retaliate and destroy the other even if it had been attacked first. This provided a deterrent for mutually assured destruction, appropriately abbreviated MAD.

We are facing an increasing danger of nuclear war, yet very little thought is given to preventing it. Again, this stands in stark contrast to the Cold War, when the best brains were devoted to studying the subject. A radically new approach is needed, and I am too much of an amateur to propose one. All the alternatives must be considered. A case can be made for total nuclear disarmament,* but I do not consider it sound because it would give too much of a chance to a rogue state to break the rules. I do believe that a regime could be devised in which the nuclear powers would drastically reduce their arsenals under international control and at the same time establish a stronger enforcement mechanism against proliferation. I may be accused of putting too

*Jonathan Schell, "The Folly of Arms Control," *Foreign Affairs*, September/October 2000, pp. 22–46.

much faith in international controls, but I do believe that they could work a lot better if the United States put its weight behind them. In any case this is not a concrete proposal, only a pointer of the direction we ought to explore. The trouble is, it would constitute too much of a break with the present situation, and it is difficult to introduce a radical change in normal times. Yet it would be tempting fate to wait until times become more abnormal.

The Bush administration is determined to perpetuate its military superiority by unilaterally pursuing NMD.* This is a feasible policy, but I consider it ill advised because it offers no defense against asymmetric threats. We cannot protect ourselves against terrorism without international cooperation. Only if people are on our side can terrorists be prevented from operating. I would have expected September 11 to give rise to second thoughts, but the Bush administration seems ideologically committed to a unilateral approach.

It may be thought from the fact that I advocate international cooperation that I am opposed to the use of military

*The Vision 2020 statement of the United States Space Command declares its goal is "dominating the space dimension of military operations to protect US interests and investment. Integrating Space Forces into war fighting capabilities across the full spectrum of conflict." See www.spacecom.af.mil/usspacecom/visbook.pdf.

force. That is not the case. I advocated military intervention in Bosnia and Kosovo, and I am glad of the extent of American military superiority. It follows from the postulate of imperfect understanding that all our efforts at crisis prevention may come to naught, and as a fallback position we had better be prepared to win military confrontations if and when they occur. But the allocation of efforts and resources to international assistance as compared to our military preparedness is completely out of proportion: $301 billion in defense expenditures* versus $10 billion in Official Development Assistance in 2000.

No regime can survive by military force alone, and the world certainly cannot be ruled by military superiority. I believe our superiority is great enough to allow us to think of other things than trying to increase it further. Unless we manage to control the proliferation of weapons of mass destruction, there is a real danger that our civilization eventually will be destroyed. If our security were threatened by other states we could not afford to do anything about this larger danger because we would have to focus on the more immediate one, but the only threats currently facing us are asymmetric ones. We cannot protect against those threats by increasing our military superiority over other states.

*The United States Office of Management and Budget (OMB), "Federal Resources in Support of National Defense," Fiscal Year 2000.

The fight against terrorism requires international cooperation and intrusive inspection. To justify intrusive inspection the United States must change its posture from
unilateral hegemony to being the leader of a multilateral
effort to protect the world against infringements of law
and order. We are no longer in a cold war situation where
being a superpower and the leader of the free world were
identical. The Bush administration came into office with a
strong determination to reinforce our superpower status
by developing NMD. But its policy was based on an out-
dated view of the world. The convenient identity of the
Cold War is no longer valid. We must also reinforce our
status as the leader of the free world. We must form a
coalition of the willing with the objective of maintaining
law and order in the world. The coalition would sponsor
international arrangements and foster internal improvements in individual countries. It would offer incentives
where possible but would not shy away from enforcement
where necessary.

The initiative has to come from the United States. It
requires a profound change of attitude, a veritable change
of heart. Such a radical change is not possible in normal
times, but these are not normal times. We have become
aware how precarious our civilization is. It does not make
sense to devote all our energies to improving our relative

position in a social system when the system itself is drifting toward disaster. The United States is the only country in the world that is in a position to initiate a change in the world order, to replace the Washington consensus with a global open society. To do so we must abandon the unthinking pursuit of narrow self-interest and give some thought to the future of humanity.*

The difference between global capitalism and a global open society is not so great. It is not an either/or alternative but merely a change of emphasis, a better balance between competition and cooperation, a reassertion of morality amid our amoral preoccupations. It would be naïve to expect a change in human nature, but humans are capable of transcending the pursuit of narrow self-interest. Indeed, they cannot live without some sense of morality. It is market fundamentalism, which holds that the social good is best served by allowing people to pursue their self-interest without any thought for the social good—the two

*Interestingly, when Gorbachev was in charge of the Soviet Union he was genuinely concerned about the survival of humanity, and he thought that he would find a willing partner in the United States. The Chernobyl nuclear disaster was a traumatic experience for the Soviet leadership and he was really worried about a bumbling bureaucracy being in control of a tool as dangerous as nuclear power. Gorbachev sponsored an International Foundation for Survival in which Andrei Sakharov participated. Gorbachev also paid up the Soviet arrears to the UN and came to the General Assembly to announce his "new vision" but his appeal was ignored by the United States.

being identical—that is a perversion of human nature. As I said previously, I consider global capitalism a distorted form of a global open society.

The vision of a global open society I have outlined here is not a practical program like the measures proposed in the previous chapters. But acting on those proposals—particularly on the SDR proposal—would be a good beginning.

Developing an Open Society Alliance will require a lot more thought and preparation. The goal of fostering open societies has to be reconciled with geopolitical necessities. A sudden shift of policy could have a destabilizing effect. I envision the Open Society Alliance not as a replacement for our current alliances but as an additional dimension of our policy. It would aim at strengthening those governments and those elements within society that seek to move toward democracy and modernity, and it would use incentives rather than penalties as its tool. Even that could prove to be a risky proposition, but we cannot afford not to take the risk. The fight against terrorism cannot succeed unless we can also project the vision of a better world. The United States must lead the fight against poverty, ignorance, and repression with the same urgency, determination, and commitment of resources as the war on terrorism.

Appendix

THE SDR PROPOSAL

It is proposed to use SDR issues to provide development assistance and public goods on a global scale. Richer countries (as defined in the IMF "transaction plan") would donate their share of new allocations; less-developed countries would add the SDRs they receive to their monetary reserves. Thus, less developed countries would benefit both directly, through an increase in their monetary reserves and indirectly, through increased international assistance.

The proposal would be implemented in two stages. In the first stage, a special SDR 21.4 billion SDR issue (approximately $27 billion), authorized by the IMF in 1997 and currently awaiting ratification by the U.S. Congress, would be approved by Congress with the proviso that the richer countries donate their allocations in accordance with certain rules.

SDR donations could be made only to pre-approved programs. Programs would include trust funds for the provision of public goods on a global scale as well as matching funds for public/private partnerships. In the first stage, the list of eligible programs would be confined to three or four specific priority areas such as public health, education, information (the "digital divide"), and reform of judicial systems. Government-sponsored poverty reduction programs would be excluded; they would be left to the IFIs.

The plan calls for the creation of an advisory board of eminent persons operating under the aegis of the IMF but independent of it. The board would be appointed on the basis of publicly stated professional qualifications and would not be subject to instructions from the governments that appointed the members. The board would establish a list of programs eligible for SDR donations and would also recommend priorities, but it would have no authority over the spending of funds. The donors would retain the right to select from the menu prepared by the board. In this way, there would be a marketlike interaction between donors and programs, supply and demand. The board would vouch for the quality of programs, and donors would be responsive to public opinion in the quality of their selections.

There would be a separate audit commission to supervise and evaluate the programs.

If the plan is successfully implemented in connection

with the one-time special issue of SDRs, the second step of the proposal is to have annual issues of SDRs along the same lines. The range of eligible programs would be expanded. Government-sponsored poverty reduction programs could also qualify, but only up to a certain limit in order to leave funds for nongovernmental channels.

The SDR proposal serves several objectives at the same time. It combines a scheme for greater international assistance with a scheme for increasing the monetary reserves of less developed countries.

The *donation scheme* would:

1. Increase the amount available for international assistance. When fully implemented, it could go a long way toward meeting the UN's 2015 development targets.

2. Ensure a more equitable distribution of the burden and eliminate the freerider problem.

3. Remove some of the deficiencies of international assistance as currently administered, notably:
   a) An independent board would ensure that the needs of the recipients take precedence over the interests of the donors.
   b) The stranglehold of intergovernmental dealings

would be broken; recipient governments could no longer act as gatekeepers.
c) Donor coordination would be enhanced.
d) Recipients would have a greater sense of ownership and involvement.
e) There would be a feedback mechanism that reinforces successes and eliminates failures.

The provision of additional *monetary reserves* would bring tangible benefits to less-developed countries quite independently of the donation plan, but the donation plan would significantly enhance the merits of SDRs as a monetary instrument. This is supported by the following arguments:

- International trade is growing at roughly double the rate of global GDP. Countries need to maintain a prudent ratio between currency reserves and imports. Less-developed countries have to set aside part of their export earnings as reserves; SDR allocations would ease that burden. Alternatively, SDR allocations would reduce their cost of borrowing. Richer countries have no need for SDRs because they have ample reserves and/or easy access to international financial markets. By donating their SDRs, richer countries would have found a good use for them.

- The needs of the poorer countries have become more acute since 1997 because emerging markets have been facing a capital drain since then.

- New SDR issues expand global liquidity and could be considered inflationary, but inflationary pressures have abated, and there is a real possibility of global deflation. Since nominal interest rates cannot be lowered below zero, traditional monetary tools lose part of their effectiveness in a deflationary environment (e.g., Japan). SDRs would be useful as a countercyclical tool especially if the richer countries are obliged to spend their allotments through donations.

.   .   .

How SDR donations should be treated in national budgets is a question to which I cannot offer an unequivocal answer. A case can be made for both alternatives. In principle, the allocation of SDRs is a bookkeeping item, but when the SDRs are donated, that is a real expenditure. That is the case for including it in the budget. But the allocation of SDRs goes to strengthen the monetary reserves—in the case of the United States, the Exchange Stabilization Fund. If an equivalent amount is then withdrawn and spent, the monetary reserves remain unaffected except for the interest obligations vis-à-vis the IMF. Central banks, or in the U.S. case, the Treasury, do not normally seek appropriations to cover changes in their foreign exchange reserves including interest earned or lost—that is the case for making the donations outside the budget. If SDRs are treated as a countercyclical tool a case can be made that the donations should pass through budgets not when SDRs are issued but when they are recalled.

In the end every country would have to make its own determination about proper budget treatment. Whoever would object to the SDR proposal on this score ought to come up with a better idea.

Index

Index